A DE GRUMMOND PRIMER

THE
PICTORIAL PRIMER.

BY GRANDFATHER LEARY.

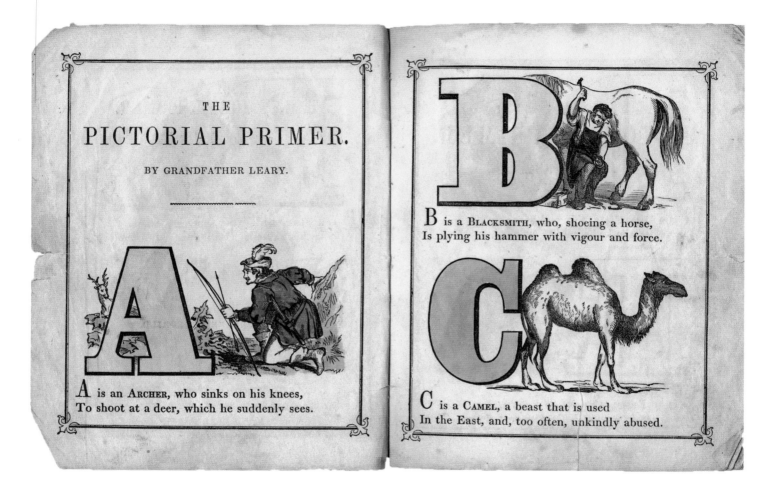

A is an ARCHER, who sinks on his knees,
To shoot at a deer, which he suddenly sees.

B is a BLACKSMITH, who, shoeing a horse,
Is plying his hammer with vigour and force.

C is a CAMEL, a beast that is used
In the East, and, too often, unkindly abused.

A DE GRUMMOND PRIMER

Highlights of the Children's Literature Collection

Edited by

Carolyn J. Brown, Ellen Hunter Ruffin, and Eric L. Tribunella

UNIVERSITY PRESS OF MISSISSIPPI / JACKSON

The University Press of Mississippi is the scholarly publishing agency of
the Mississippi Institutions of Higher Learning: Alcorn State University,
Delta State University, Jackson State University, Mississippi State University,
Mississippi University for Women, Mississippi Valley State University,
University of Mississippi, and University of Southern Mississippi.

www.upress.state.ms.us

Designed by Peter D. Halverson

The University Press of Mississippi is a member
of the Association of University Presses.

Frontispiece: First pages from *The Pictorial Primer* (1846).
Courtesy of the de Grummond Collection.

First printing 2021
∞

Library of Congress Cataloging-in-Publication Data available

ISBN 9781496833396 (hardcover)
ISBN 9781496833402 (epub single)
ISBN 9781496833419 (epub institutional)
ISBN 9781496833426 (pdf single)
ISBN 9781496833433 (pdf institutional)

British Library Cataloging-in-Publication Data available

The editors and the University Press of Mississippi wish to thank the following individuals for their generous support of this publication:

David Bogosian
Iris Easterling
Barbara Jane Foote
Susan Jones
Aubrey K. Lucas
Patsy H. Perritt
Dr. and Mrs. J. Larry Smith
Sarah and Ted Webb
Anonymous donor

Contents

Foreword

Ellen Hunter Ruffin

The de Grummond Children's Literature Collection . . . it is a mouthful to say. The de Grummond is difficult to describe because it is not just one thing.

It's an archive. It's a library. It is a library with "museum tendencies." It *is* a treasure trove, a place where one can discover books from long ago. However, it's so much more than those trite descriptive phrases.

Dr. Lena Y. de Grummond began the Collection in 1966. She was teaching children's literature to graduate students—students who were working during the day and attending class at night. Dr. de Grummond wanted to expand the textbook. She wanted her students to have an understanding of the craft of children's books. She began writing letters to authors and illustrators asking them for bits and pieces of their work to add to the "children's collection." The letter campaign didn't end with those introductory letters. She developed actual relationships with the people she wrote. When examining the correspondence from the authors and illustrators, one learns about their families, their vacations, their work projects. Dr. de Grummond was *interested* in their lives. Warm friendships evolved as a result. There's the word—"warm."

That thread has carried throughout the years of the de Grummond Collection. Dr. de Grummond's warmth seemed to imprint on the succeeding curators and assistant curators. We count it as a privilege to receive an author's life work. What they send varies, but it all points to the development of the end product—a book. Illustrators send "dummies," which are as interesting as the final art. Authors send manuscripts and typescripts edited by their editors—often adding to the story. Sometimes contributors to the Collection send personal correspondence that reveals the network of relationships between fellow authors and illustrators. One such letter in the Collection was written by Esphyr Slobodkina and sent to her friend, Margaret Wise Brown. Slobodkina expresses her frustration with the lack of support she receives from her publisher. She writes a "practice letter" to her publisher, and at the top of the page, she asks her friend, "Margaret, should I send this?" Margaret Wise Brown replies, "Phyra, I suggest you get two bottles of red wine and start a roaring fire using this for kindling."

It is impossible to ignore the books in the Collection. A primer is an introductory book on a subject, but also a book used to teach children how to read that often includes a variety of texts drawn from different aspects of children's culture. Our *Primer* will introduce you to fairy tales, to early books for children, and to a broad range of early titles. The de Grummond Collection tells the story of the history of children's literature. The earliest imprint is a 1530 Aesop's Fables, written before the idea of a literature specific to children was a reality. We also have contemporary books—both fiction and nonfiction. The series books are a signature of the Collection. Along with G. A. Henty, Horatio Alger, Nancy Drew, and Trixie Belden, we have the complete series of Martha Finley's Elsie Dinsmore books. Publishers fill in the gaps by sending new books, advanced readers' copies, and folded and gathered picture books (F&Gs), which continue to tell a story about book production.

The scholars who have willingly contributed to the book deserve monumental thanks. Of course, we wanted to tell Dr. Lena Y. de Grummond's story, which Carolyn Brown has accomplished. Dr. Brown's observations of the hesitation of some authors to send their work to Mississippi in 1966 emphasize sensitive times and feelings during the era of the Collection's founding. One of the goals with this primer was to give an understanding of the breadth of the de Grummond Collection. One of the foremost scholars of fairy tales, Ruth B. Bottigheimer, gives a quick history of fairy tales, and she emphasizes what scholars can find for research.

Whom better could we have asked than Laura Wasowicz, the curator of children's literature at the American Antiquarian Society, to discuss the earliest forms used in teaching children to read? Wasowicz offers a concise description of hornbooks, battledores, and chapbooks contained in the Collection.

In chapter 4, Paige Gray examines the early children's readers and primers held in the de Grummond. The differences in the materials during the American Civil War are distinct. While some books are printed in Boston, others are printed in Charleston—depicting differing regional values.

Alexandra Valint, in chapter 5, "The Golden Age of Illustrated Children's Books," examines children's literature available in the mid-nineteenth century. Illustrations transitioned from caricature to a more realistic, painterly style, as evidenced in the works of classic children's book illustrators such Walter Crane, Kate Greenaway, Randolph Caldecott, and others.

Amy Pattee brings her passion for series fiction to her essay about the evolution of series fiction for youth. Her descriptions of Jacob Abbott's Rollo series give a glimpse of the roots of contemporary series, currently popular with youngsters.

One hallmark of the de Grummond Collection is the commitment to multiple editions of books. Eric Tribunella writes of the multiple editions of a single work as a source interest for readers of children's literature. For example, the de Grummond Collection holds more than fifty copies of Frances Hodgson Burnett's *The Secret Garden* and Louisa May Alcott's *Little Women*. Tribunella's explanation of the significance of various editions of a single title emphasizes the strengths of research in de Grummond.

Lorinda Cohoon discusses the significant collection of children's periodicals available at the de Grummond and emphasizes the usefulness of nineteenth-century children's periodicals in examining key details about the culture of the day. These periodicals, such as the popular *St. Nicholas* and *Girl's Own Paper*, give glimpses of an evolving understanding of childhood through the centuries and decades. Megan Norcia's chapter on dolls, toys, toy books, and games highlights other elements of children's culture contained in the Collection and examines the close relationship between children's books and the material artifacts of childhood. Norcia demonstrates how a study of children's toys and games provides an important window into the construction of childhood and the education of children.

In chapter 10, Nathalie op de Beeck offers an overview of the picture book. She addresses the precursors of picture books and discusses how they evolved over the course of the twentieth century into their present form. The interdependence of words and pictures work to capture children's interests and come to define the form. Op de Beeck speaks of how a picture book can take a child reader "from instruction to delight."

Chapter 11, written jointly by Jennifer Brannock and Andrew Haley, gives us an interesting examination of nonfiction and its significance in a collection like de Grummond. Children's nonfiction has changed over the decades, and the de Grummond Collection makes it possible for scholars to gain insight into the past by examining how nonfiction books represented the world to girls and boys.

Deborah Taylor's chapter on African American literature and writers provides a concise historical perspective on the struggle of finding true and positive images of Black children. Taylor discusses the different sides of the issue when she mentions Augusta Baker's question, "Are books providing positive identification for black children? Are white children seeing a true picture of the ethnic, cultural, and historical aspects of black Americans?"

Laura Hakala's chapter on southern children's literature sheds light on the unique differences between books written in the North and those written in the South. While there is a shared didacticism in the early books, there is a notable difference in the South, especially in terms of early southern literature's treatment of racial and regional identities. Hakala also discusses southern periodicals and their influence on children.

Ramona Caponegro discusses contemporary writers and the de Grummond's significant manuscript collection, including the papers of contemporary young adult writers like Angela Johnson and John Green. As Caponegro explains, the major changes in children's literature in the contemporary period have come to be associated with the rise of New Realism in the 1960s and the growth of the children's and young adult literature markets. No topic is now taboo.

Anita Silvey's chapter 15 speaks of the onset of quality and inexpensive children's books, which made good books accessible to many children. Beginning in 1942, the Golden Books sold for twenty-five cents in the marketplace, and one of those little books became the best-selling children's book in the world: *The Poky Little Puppy*.

While serving as the collection specialist in the de Grummond, Ann Mulloy Ashmore saw the H. A. and Margret Rey Papers arrive. As a result of her introduction to the Reys, Ashmore became a Rey scholar, and her essay on the Rey Papers in the Collection describe a virtual playground for researchers. Rudine Sims Bishop's essay on the Ezra Jack Keats Papers at de Grummond speaks to the significance of his Caldecott-winning book *The Snowy Day*. Bishop gives an overview of the Keats Papers and the Keats Foundation. She discusses all of Keats's characters, and how the work of Keats, beginning with Peter, continued to show a multicultural world.

It would have been impossible to discuss every named collection in de Grummond because there are so many (over 1,300); therefore, in chapter 18, selected friends of the Collection speak to a few of the notable examples. Allison Kaplan presents the findings of her research in the Tana Hoban Papers. She describes Hoban's work in children's literature, as well as her accomplished career in photography. Following Tana Hoban is the noted cartoonist and children's author, Syd Hoff. His niece, Carol Edmonston, provides a glimpse of the remarkable work of her uncle. Hoff is followed by Tasha Tudor in a contribution by John Hare. Hare's familiarity with the Tudor Collection at de Grummond comes from his experience as a bibliographer of Tudor's work. Longtime friend of Richard Peck and editor of *The Horn Book*, Roger Sutton, does not attempt to mask his appreciation of Peck's ability to draw memorable and humorous characters. Fans of James Marshall's work will enjoy reading Danielle Bishop Stoulig's contribution on him. Stoulig, former assistant curator at the de Grummond Collection, has the advantage of having worked with Marshall's papers for many years.

Finally, my coeditors and I imagined this volume as showcasing the de Grummond Collection to readers interested in learning about the history of children's literature as reflected in the Collection's holdings, as well as to scholars seeking to learn more about the research possibilities of de

Grummond. We are especially proud to bring together researchers who approach the study of children's literature from different disciplinary perspectives, from librarians and archivists to literary critics. *A de Grummond Primer* is the first book devoted to Lena de Grummond's extraordinary contribution to the state of Mississippi, which now draws scholars from around the world seeking to study in one of the largest children's literature archives in North America. As you will discover in the essays that follow, what makes de Grummond unique is the breadth of its holdings, from historical children's books and contemporary literature and scholarship to its vast collection of original manuscripts and illustrations. *A de Grummond Primer* provides an introduction to the vast holdings that constitute the Collection.

A de Grummond Primer

Chapter 1

LENA DE GRUMMOND AND THE FOUNDING OF THE COLLECTION

Carolyn J. Brown

What does one do after retirement? Is it an end or a beginning? In my case it was a beginning.

—LENA DE GRUMMOND, from "Growth of an Idea: The de Grummond Collection"

In 1969, four years after Dr. Lena de Grummond joined the faculty of the University of Southern Mississippi, an article declared her as the woman with "the Midas touch," suggesting that the children's literature collection she founded at the university came effortlessly and was both highly regarded and valued as a treasure (Lambou 7). The mythological allusion and its connotations are apt in describing a woman whose life was devoted to books, primarily children's literature, but the reference downplays de Grummond's years of hard work and service, which preceded the founding of this priceless collection. The de Grummond Collection is a treasure, due entirely to one woman's painstaking efforts over several years.

Lena Young was born on 7 April 1900 in Centreville, Louisiana, to William J. and Amy Etienne Young. She was one of nine children; her siblings were Eugene, Pearl, William J., Alma, Karl Etienne, George, Maimie, and Lee Jacob. Not much is known of her early life, but she married prior to attending college at the University of Louisiana at Lafayette (formerly

Facing page: An undated photograph of Lena de Grummond. Courtesy of the de Grummond Collection.

Southwestern Louisiana Institute), earning her undergraduate degree in 1929. Her husband, William ("Will") White de Grummond, was an engineer with the US Corps of Engineers ("Dr. Lena Young de Grummond" 2). They had two children: Jewel Lynne and William White ("Bill") Jr. ("Biographical Sketch," de Grummond and Delaune Papers). Shortly after Bill's birth, Will died in a "tragic drowning accident" ("Dr. Lena Young de Grummond" 2).

De Grummond raised her children on her own and returned to school, entering Louisiana State University at Baton Rouge to earn a second bachelor's degree in library science in 1937. It would be this degree that would set de Grummond on her path; she would forge a career that encompassed all levels of library science, first serving as a librarian in both Sulphur and Houma, Louisiana; then working for the Louisiana State Library Commission; and finally being named State Supervisor of School Libraries for Louisiana for sixteen years (Arnold 6). According to Anne Lundin, former assistant curator of the de Grummond Collection, "Dr. de Grummond worked in Louisiana for many years in various aspects of librarianship and teaching: a staff member of the Louisiana State Library, a high school teacher-librarian, and, until her retirement in 1965, a state supervisor of school libraries for fifteen years" (1). A lifelong student, during her tenure as state supervisor of school libraries, she returned to Louisiana State University and earned her doctorate in library science, graduating in 1956, the same year her son, Bill, and future daughter-in-law, Nancy, both earned their undergraduate degrees as well (Leeper 13).

In 1965 de Grummond faced a situation with which many are familiar: forced retirement at age sixty-five. In her essay, "Growth of an Idea: The de Grummond Collection," de Grummond writes: "When I was told that the newly-elected Superintendent of Education wanted all staff members who could retire to do so, I knew there must be another right place for me to serve, and I prayed for guidance. My prayer was answered rather promptly by two offers of positions teaching graduate library science" (1). The choice she made is now the stuff of children's literature legend, as she decided to go to work for the University of Southern Mississippi in Hattiesburg. She recalls that decision in the same essay: "I considered academic matters very carefully, but one of the factors that influenced my choice was a statement by my son. While at L.S.U. he had attended a classical fraternity conference at the University of Southern Mississippi and said, 'Mother, the campus is very attractive and so is Hattiesburg. I'm sure you would be happy there.' I am, for beauty helps to bring happiness" (2).

In 1965 Lena de Grummond began her teaching career at the University of Southern Mississippi. She taught a children's literature class that met once a week at night for four hours. De Grummond describes those first classes: "My classes were all taught at night—such fine classes, composed of school people who worked at their jobs all day, drove to a four-hour class (some coming more than 100 miles each way), and then drove back to be ready for work [the] next day. Such students are surely worthy of all the enrichment a teacher can give" (2). Because her days were mostly free, she writes that she "gave earnest thought to what [she] could do for [her] students" (2). It was then that she recalled as state supervisor of libraries in Louisiana that she had met or knew "a number of authors and illustrators of children's books" (2). This knowledge prompted her to begin a letter-writing campaign to authors and artists of children's books, explaining about her desire to build a collection "for use by teachers and librarians" (2).

In 1970, when she looked back at the early days of building the collection in her essay "Growth of an Idea: The de Grummond Collection," she described her epistolary process:

> I wrote . . . all letters in longhand. Sometimes I wrote 400 to 500 letters a week, but usually 100 was average. I explained my project and said we were buying copies of their books (we were) but lacked those materials which enrich a collection, such as original illustrations, manuscripts of published books, dummies, sketches, etc., and simply asked, "Would you like to help us with some of yours?" (2–3)

De Grummond's description of her letter does not do the actual letter justice. The actual letter that she sent is quoted below (de Grummond to Matulay, 18 May 1966), and particular phrases and sentiments in her appeal moved many authors and illustrators to respond. The letter was sent on University of Southern Mississippi letterhead:

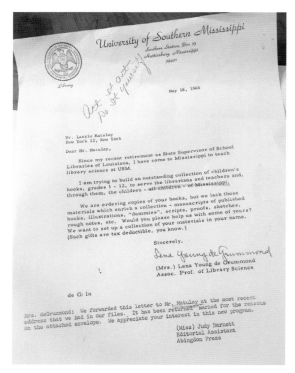

An example of Lena de Grummond's original collection letter, sent to artist and illustrator Laszlo Matulay in 1966. Courtesy of the de Grummond Collection.

Dear   ,

Since my recent retirement as State Supervisor of School Libraries of Louisiana, I have come to Mississippi to teach library science at USM.

I am trying to build an outstanding collection of children's books, grades 1–12, to serve the librarians and teachers, and, through them, the children—all children—of Mississippi.

We are ordering copies of your books, but we lack those materials which enrich a collection—manuscripts of published books, illustrations, "dummies," scripts, proofs, sketches, rough notes, etc. Would you please help us with some of yours? We want to set up a collection of your materials in your name. (Such gifts are tax deductible, you know.)

Sincerely,

(Mrs.) Lena Young de Grummond
Assoc. Prof. of Library Science

Based on the plethora of responses, two sentiments in de Grummond's letter stand out and spoke to many of the authors and illustrators: first, the fact that she pointed out that her new collection was intended to not only "serve the librarians and teachers" of Mississippi, but "through them, the children—*all* [my italics] children of Mississippi"; and the second was casually mentioned in the parenthetical comment at the end of the letter: "(Such gifts are tax deductible, you know)."

In the mid-sixties, when de Grummond sent her earliest letters, Mississippi was at the epicenter of many of the most horrific and tragic events of the civil rights movement. In May 1963, a faculty member and a group of students from Tougaloo College were beaten and arrested when they sat down at the lunch counter at Woolworth's in downtown Jackson; this incident was followed by the murder in June of Medgar Evers, secretary of the Mississippi NAACP, in the front yard of his home. These heinous crimes were followed the next year with the discovery of the bodies of three civil rights workers, two white, one black, near Philadelphia, Mississippi. James E. Chaney, twenty-one; Andrew Goodman, twenty-one;

and Michael Schwerner, twenty-four, had been working to register black voters, and on 21 June they went to investigate the burning of a black church. They were arrested by the police on speeding charges, incarcerated for several hours, and released after dark into the hands of the Ku Klux Klan, who murdered them. With many of these abominable crimes on Americans' minds, one Mississippi woman's efforts to do something good for "all children—of Mississippi" spoke directly to the hearts and minds of writers and illustrators of many nationalities and religions.

Perhaps the author who said it best in his reply to de Grummond's letter was H. Arthur Klein, a writer who lived in California and, with his wife, Mina, wrote children's books on a wide array of subjects: "They collaborate[d] on most of their books, except for those about science, which Mr. Klein wrote and Mrs. Klein helped to edit. . . . In addition to books on science, Mr. Klein wrote a book about surfing, and with his wife, edited an anthology about surfing. Together, they have written about Jewish history and fine art" ("Biographical Sketch," Klein Papers). After describing his books to de Grummond, he concludes his letter (3 January 1966) with this paragraph:

> *There is one other question of much importance to me personally. Your letter emphasizes the phrase all children of Mississippi. I could not in good conscience make presentations of material that has been so important in my working life, if it were to be maintained in a collection inaccessible to teachers or pupils on the basis of skin pigmentation, religious preference, or backgrounds, or ethnic differences. As a writer I do my best to make important knowledge available to all children who have interest in it, and I would like even the husks of my books—the mss, etc.—repose under unsegregated conditions. I am sure you will understand my concern.*
>
> *Sincerely yours,*
>
> *H. Arthur Klein*

Letter from H. Arthur Klein to Lena de Grummond from 3 January 1966. Courtesy of the de Grummond Collection.

De Grummond clearly pacified Klein's concerns because in the Collection today are seven of Klein's books, as well as many "husks": typescripts, galleys, proofs, and dummies.

Another writer, Lois S. Johnson, also expressed concern over donating materials to a Mississippi school that had barred admittance to a young African American man. She wrote de Grummond (3 August 1966) that she had read an article from 8 November 1962, about Clyde Kennard, which told of his "repeated attempts . . . to be admitted as a student, and of his failures every step of the way." Johnson writes de Grummond that she realizes "that in the five years since the publication of this article, many changes have been made" and was reassured by de Grummond's reply:

> The fact that you wrote that you had Negroes enrolled in your classes shows clearly that the segregation policy has been changed in your University. You show your own broadmindedness when you wrote me that you "teach all alike—with no bonus to anyone for being a member of any race." That is the way all teachers should feel toward all their pupils.

Through her solicitation letter, de Grummond unintentionally served to help Mississippi redefine itself to those whose impression of the state was extremely negative.

The second carrot that de Grummond offered at the conclusion of her letter excited many of the writers and illustrators that she contacted initially: that contributions to the Collection would be tax deductible. According to Emily Murphy in "Unpacking the Archive: Value, Pricing, and the Letter-Writing Campaign of Dr. Lena Y. de Grummond," de Grummond's offer of a tax deduction came at an excellent time:

> During this period, she won many an author and illustrator over by providing generous assessments of the economic value of donated materials that could then be used to reduce the donor's taxes. This tactic for increasing the number of collection contributions was not, of course, unique to the de Grummond collection. Rather, it represented one of the few legal avenues for children's literature collections

to provide some form of financial compensation to their contributors. As de Grummond's letters reveal, the promise of tax deductions not only increased the number of donations the collection received, it also increased the economic value of these materials. Even after the US government altered the tax code in 1969 and made such transactions illegal, many of de Grummond's donors remained loyal to her. (553)

Many authors and artists had no idea that their earliest drafts and sketches held any intrinsic value or interest to others, but de Grummond assured them that all these materials were worth saving and donating. She states in her essay, "Growth of an Idea," "I have suggested facetiously at times, 'If you put your materials in the trash basket, please mail the basket to us'" (3).

Thus, the letter-writing campaign began, and de Grummond's earliest epistolary requests resulted in great gains for both her students and the university. The first to respond and accept were Berta and Elmer Hader, highly regarded children's book authors and illustrators who collaborated on many projects, including *The Big Snow*, which won the Caldecott medal in 1948.

De Grummond started her letter-writing campaign in January 1966. The Hader's reply must have brought her great joy, for it is a letter to treasure. Not only did they respond quickly and positively, but the letter is one-of-a-kind; originally decorated in the Haders' trademark art and style:

January 28th;
1966:

Lena Y. de Grummond
University of Southern Mississippi
Hattiesburg, Mississippi

Dear Lena Y. de Grummond:

We received your letter of January 18th; telling us that you were building up an outstanding collection of Children's Books for the University of Southern Mississippi and asking us to contribute some original material. We will be very happy to send you a manuscript

ELMER S. HADER
55 RIVER ROAD
NYACK, NEW YORK 10960

January 28th;
1 9 6 6

Mr. Ground Hog

Lena Y. de Grummond
University of Southern Mississippi
Hattiesburg, Mississippi

Dear Lena Y. de Grummond:

We received your letter of January 18th;
telling us that you were building up an outstanding
collection of Children's Books for the University
of Southern Mississippi and asking us to contribute
some original material. We will be very happy to send
you a manuscript and some illustrations from one of
our books, as soon as we have time to look over the
material on hand.

You mentioned in your letter that our books
are popular in Louisiana and we thought you might have
a particular title in mind for your collection of
original material. If so, please let us know.

Mrs. Hader joins me in all good wishes.

Sincerely,

Berta and Elmer Hader

(Left) Letter from Berta and Elmer Hader to Lena de Grummond from
28 January 1966. Courtesy of the de Grummond Collection.

(Right) Letter from Berta and Elmer Hader to Lena de Grummond from
14 March 1966. Courtesy of the de Grummond Collection.

ELMER S. HADER
55 RIVER ROAD
NYACK, NEW YORK 10960

UNIVERSITY OF
SOUTHERN MISSISSIPPI

March 14th;
1 9 6 6

Dear Mrs. de Grummond:

Under separate cover we are sending
you all the manuscripts for DING-DONG-BELL, from the
very first idea for the book to the final typed copy.
As you will see, the title was changed several times
before we settled on DING-DONG-BELL. We do not always
rewrite so much, however, we thought you would like to
know just what we did in the way of working out the idea.

We have also sent you all the dummys
for this book, from the first rough thought sketches
to the final work dummy with the galley proofs of the
book pasted in place. In addition we are sending you
several of the color illustrations and two of the
black and white drawings and the design for the book
jacket. Also with the dummys we are including an
autographed copy of the book and our Christmas greeting
for the year the book was published.

Your grandchildren must be a joy to
you and we know how happy you must be that their father
is back safe and sound from Vietnam. We are happy too.
Williamsburg is such a charming place. We hope you will
be able to visit your family there.

We have no children of our own but
we know how you feel about your grandchildren. We have
nieces and nephews and lovely young grand neices and
nephews to delight us.

We are glad to know that you liked
our stationery because we made the little sketch on
it just for you. All good wishes to you and to your
work in Library Science at the University of Southern
Mississippi.

Sincerely,

Berta and Elmer Hader

Ans. 3-24-66 (3000)

and some illustrations from one of our books, as soon as we have time
to look over the materials on hand. . . .
Mrs. Hader joins me in all good wishes.

Sincerely,

Berta and Elmer Hader

In less than two months' time, the Haders responded with another delightfully decorated letter, informing de Grummond that they would be sending "Under separate cover . . . all the manuscripts for DING-DONG-BELL from the very first idea to the final typed copy. As you will see, the title was changed several times before we settled on DING-DONG-BELL. We do not always rewrite so much, however, we thought you would like to know just what we did in the way of working out an idea" (14 March 1966). This second letter also reveals how quickly de Grummond warmed to her correspondents; the Haders' reply, after archival business is concluded, shares information about their personal life, and they illustrate the masthead of the letter with a cheerful feline making its way to Hattiesburg:

We have no children of our own but we know how you feel about
your grandchildren. We have nieces and nephews and lovely young
grand neices [sic] and nephews to delight us.
We are glad to know that you liked our stationery because we made
the little sketch on it just for you. All good wishes to you and to your
work in Library Science at the University of Southern Mississippi.

Sincerely,

Berta and Elmer Hader

The first year of de Grummond's letter-writing campaign resulted in other remarkable responses during 1966, including H. A. Rey, Madeleine L'Engle, Garth Williams, Lois Lenski, and J. R. R. Tolkien. On 1 March 1966, Garth Williams, the famous artist of E. B. White's *Stuart Little* and

Charlotte's Web, who lived in Guanajuato, Mexico, replied that he would look for an item or two to send, but his letter seems to speak for all artists (he uses the collective pronoun "we"), and his final sentence, written over fifty years ago, seem prescient:

> *I shall look for "something" to add to your library collection. Unfortunately, originals are either kept by the publisher—or kept for hopeful sales. However I make an incredible number of quick rough impressions of a scene I am about to illustrate, and perhaps I can dig up a handful to show that we really do a lot of unseen work—us poor illustrators. Sometimes I make over 50 studies for a new character, and mull over them for months; even years nowadays.*
>
> *I sincerely hope you have the greatest success in your project as the importance of books grows with able hands from your librarians,—or they fail for want of your training in library science. Ultimately, for the want of a book, can the nation be lost.*
>
>

very sincerely [sic],

Garth Williams.

Immediately following Williams's reply was the first letter from H. A. Rey (20 April 1966), which would result in one of the largest and most important collections in the de Grummond today. Rey decorates his stationery, like the Haders did, with a wonderful illustration of Curious George making his way to Hattiesburg. Rey tells de Grummond that he has sent her the following, which will be the first of many contributions that the Reys make to de Grummond over the next thirty years:

> *In a separate mailing tube I am sending you an autographed proof sheet of "C.G. goes to the Hospital" and a star chart, and enclosed goes an autobiographical folder, a set of miniature book jackets, a photo of author plus monkey (it isn't george [sic] but a borrowed little chimpanzee girl), a fan-mail-answering card, and our last year's and this year's New Year's card—and also a small rough sketch of george [sic] about to swallow a piece of jig-saw puzzle.*

Letter from the Reys with Curious George making his way to Hattiesburg, 20 April 1966. Courtesy of the de Grummond Collection.

Rey's response was followed two months later by another famous author/illustrator whose contributions to children's literature and support of the de Grummond Collection would earn her the first ever University of Southern Mississippi Medallion in 1969. Lois Lenski (6 May 1966) responded to de Grummond's first request quite generously and continued to send materials over the years:

> Dear Mrs. de Grummond:
> Yesterday I shipped to you one large package and one book parcel by insured parcel post. These contain the nucleus of your Lois Lenski Collection—assorted illustrations from various books, foreign editions and a few other books you might not otherwise find, and various articles by and about myself and my work and varied miscellaneous items; all listed in detail on the enclosed sheets.

Lenski's friendship with de Grummond and others at the university revealed an extensive correspondence that includes much that is personal, such as expressions of concern over Hurricane Camille in 1969, in addition to archival matters.

Not all responses resulted in treasures, but sometimes the letter is itself the treasure. On 15 August 1966, J. R. R. Tolkien replied to de

PROFESSOR J. R. R. TOLKIEN

OXFORD 61639

76 SANDFIELD ROAD
HEADINGTON
OXFORD

15th August, 1966.

Dear Mrs. Young de Grummond,

　　Thank you very much for your letter.
I am interested to hear of your plan to form
a collection of children's books and am, of
course, pleased to hear that I shall be included.
I am afraid, however, that I have not anything
to contribute in the way of manuscripts or
sketches. For one thing, I am very busy at
the moment writing and have not the time to
do the necessary sorting and examination of
material. In any case I have practically
decided now, in view of the high value that
these items are acquiring, to bequeath all
that I still retain to my literary executor
for the benefit of my own family.

　　　　With best wishes,

　　　　　　Yours sincerely,

Mrs. L. Young de Grummond,
The University öf Southern Mississippi,
Southern Station, Box 313,
Hattiesburg,
Mississippi 39401,
U.S.A.

J. R. R. Tolkien's unsigned letter to Lena de Grummond, 15 August 1966. Courtesy of the de Grummond Collection.

Grummond's request, but surprisingly answered that he had nothing to contribute:

> Dear Mrs. Young de Grummond:
> 　Thank you very much for your letter. I am interested to hear of your plan to form a collection of children's books and am, of course, pleased to hear that I shall be included. I am afraid, however, that I have not anything to contribute in the way of manuscripts or sketches. For one thing, I am very busy at the moment writing and have not the time to do the necessary sorting and examination of material. In any case I have practically decided now, in view of the high value that these items are acquiring, to bequeath all that I still retain to my literary executor for the benefit of my own family.
>
> 　　　With best wishes,
>
> 　　　Yours sincerely,

Tolkien forgets to sign his letter, and exactly two months later de Grummond receives a second note from Tolkien, apologizing for failing to sign the first and promising if he has "a moment to spare . . . [to] find some item or items for you." De Grummond never did receive any sketches or drafts from the creative genius behind *The Lord of the Rings*, but at least she has two letters by this brilliant scholar to include in her burgeoning collection.

Madeleine L'Engle also responded (24 October 1966), and her reply is very revealing in that it provides a glimpse into both her personal life and her writing process. She also is quite excited by the fact that her contributions may be considered tax deductible. Although she had already found literary success (*A Wrinkle in Time* was published in 1962), she tells de Grummond she has three children who will all soon be attending college and every little bit helps:

> Dear Mrs. de Grummond,
> 　. . . I never do a book in less than three drafts and it usually runs to more than that, at least for large sections. Rewriting is really the

main work of a book for me. I sometimes write in bed with a pencil or pen, and when I type I use the back of the rejects to write letters on to close friends and family who know my Scot feelings about wasting paper! But there is always lots left over. So let me know, please, just exactly what you would like, and I will do my best to get it to you.

And one question, please: how can such a gift be tax-deductible? Since we have three teenagers all of whom will be going to college any tax help interests us!

I'm enclosing a rejected page from a lecture to see if this is at all the kind of thing that you are looking for.

Sincerely,

Madeleine L'Engle

A letter to a Miss Rosenbaum (13 July 1968) that L'Engle shares with de Grummond is a fascinating document that shines a light on L'Engle's home life and her scientific background, definitely the type of material de Grummond is attempting to obtain. The letter describes a chaotic household with L'Engle's eighty-seven-year-old mother living with her, who, she writes, "is very much a dowager, duchess, demanding, domineering, difficult, and, when she wants to be, charming"; her eldest daughter, her daughter's husband, and their three-week-old baby; as well as an assortment of cats, dogs, and even birds! She also reveals that her husband, Hugh Franklin, is "off making a movie."

Her paragraph about the science behind *A Wrinkle in Time* also is worth quoting in its entirety:

Your question about science: I was good at conceptual science at school and very bad at practical science; higher math makes more sense to me than arithmetic, at which I'm still poor. I don't really quite know how I got going on the science which comes into Wrinkle, Starfish, and Unicorns—mostly it was the bigger ideas behind the books which led to the more specific research I did on science. While I was writing Wrinkle I was reading a good deal of theology, plus contemporary

physics and cosmology. Now that we have a theologian "in the family"
[her son-in-law] I've got to know and become friends with a good
many eminent theologians—and of course our dinner table often
stimulates conversations that turn up in my books.

L'Engle's letter is an example of the correspondence de Grummond must have been thrilled to receive as she dedicated herself to acquiring materials for the Collection.

Over the next two years the replies and contributions multiplied, and authors often would send materials without having to be asked. On 11 November 1967 cartoonist and children's book author Syd Hoff wrote to the Collection, asking if there was interest in "some drawings of mine, from my daily newspaper panel 'LAUGH IT OFF' syndicated in about a hundred cities here and abroad through King Features." He based his inquiry on the fact that he had contributed to the Collection the year before. Lois Lenski sends another shipment, and writer Helen Orlob not only sends an original manuscript, but also asks de Grummond if she would have interest in thirty archival photos that were not used in her book, *Daring Young Men in the Flying Machines,* but are "copies of very old photos, obtained with a great deal of trouble" (30 October 1967). In 1968 the voluntary contributions continue with author Leo Schneider offering four unsolicited manuscripts, as well as Gertrude Warner, author of the Boxcar series, sending "miscellaneous mss and original notebooks" (4 January 1968). In order to keep up with the myriad of letters and items arriving each day, de Grummond maintained a unique system of notebooks to manage the correspondence she was having with authors, illustrators, agents, editors, and publishers in the field of children's literature.

De Grummond's notebooks provide a compelling glimpse into her mind, the mind of someone who is acutely skilled in library science and, therefore, recordkeeping. Each notebook represents one year or part of a year over several years of time, and each page of each notebook is given to one writer and one writer only. The notebook pages are alphabetized by the last name of the correspondent. Each entry looks very much like the example below; written in de Grummond's own hand, the entry starts with the author or artist's name listed first, followed by his or her address,

Apartado Postal 123.
Guanajuato, Guanajuato, Mexic[o]
March 1st. 1966

Mrs Lena Young d[e] [...]

Bond, Michael   5 Lion Close
   Telephone 0428-4614   Haslemere
Paddington at work: Surrey, England
  16 rough sketches:
  final corrected typescript

A Bear Called Paddington (1960)
  1 set galley proofs.
Here Comes Thursday (ill. by Daphne Rowles)
  1 publ copy (sent by Lippincott)

        on Haslemere
0428-   4614

Phoned June 27 - wanted me to come to
visit them, but I can't spare the time, He [1971]
will come in on Monday, July 5, at 11 a.m.,
to take me to lunch.
   Michael came promptly and we had a
fine visit. In a way, he reminds me of
Len Kessler. I gave him Janina Edes'
name and address, as he is interested
in an illustrator (he doesn't draw).
  He, Mrs Bond, + Karen (now 13) will
probably come to U.S. by way of New Orleans.
Will also go to San Francisco + New York.
  (Suggested Janina Ede)

A page from Lena de Grummond's notebook
with notes about her correspondence with
Michael Bond, creator of Paddington Bear.
Courtesy of the de Grummond Collection.

list of works, and significant details about each correspondent garnered from a letter or phone call:

> *Sobol, Donald J.*
> *Coral Gables 33143*
> *Newest address is c/o Thos. Nelson, Publ.*
> *Encyclopedia Brown and the Case of the Secret Pitch*
> *c.c. ms. & galley proofs*
> *Home address (8–27–71)*
> *12505 Vista Lane, Miami, Fla. 33156*
>
> *Give regards from Mildred Lawrence*
> *Tried to get him twice—unsuccessfully*
> *(note)*
> *Had a visit over phone—very satisfactory—friend of Jerry & Vivian Rosen*

No one is exempt from this recordkeeping system; from Michael Bond, author of the Paddington books to de Grummond's own daughter, Lynn. In fact, even though Lynn is de Grummond's daughter, her notebook page looks just like Donald Sobol's; it provides her address as well as a list of her books, several of which de Grummond herself collaborated on with her. It also contains a biographical entry (many of the entries do), which reveals that her daughter followed in her mother's footsteps and obtained a graduate degree in library science from Louisiana State University.

What makes de Grummond so uniquely positioned to start the Collection that bears her name is not only the fact that she was a librarian and teacher, but also that she was an author of children's books herself. De Grummond wrote *How to Have What You Want in Your Future* in 1959, and co-wrote, with her daughter Lynn Delaune, four biographies for children: *Jeff Davis, Confederate Boy* (1960); *Jeb Stuart* (1962); *Babe Didrikson: Girl Athlete* (1963); and *Jean Felix Piccard: Boy Balloonist* (1968) ("Biographical Sketch," de Grummond and Delaune Papers). De Grummond understood the writing process, especially the writing of children's nonfiction, and even gave her own research materials from three of her

(Left) Lena de Grummond and university librarian Warren Tracy at the first Children's Book Festival in 1968. Courtesy of the de Grummond Collection.

(Right) Lois Lenski receiving Children's Literature Medallion at the second Children's Book Festival in 1969, with Warren Tracy, university librarian (on left), and William D. McCain, university president (on right). Courtesy of the de Grummond Collection.

books to her Collection. The de Grummond Collection website states that "The de Grummond/Delaune Papers contain material for three books, *Jean Felix Piccard: Boy Balloonist*; *Jeb Stuart*; and *Jeff Davis, Confederate Boy*, which Ms. de Grummond co-wrote with her daughter, Lynne Delaune. The Collection contains research notes, a manuscript, and a typescript for this title" ("Scope and Content"). Her participation in the process gives her credibility and a genuine connection to those with whom she corresponded. That fact is borne out when she writes in "Growth of an Idea" that "Through this project we have made friends. Where answers to letters used to start 'Dear Dr. de Grummond' [or] 'Dear Professor de Grummond,' they often start now with 'Dear Lena,' and give me welcome news of family members, births, coming weddings, and other events such as new books, awards, etc., as well as the passing on of loved ones. They also write that they are encouraged by our interest and affection. No friends could be dearer to me" (3).

De Grummond's vision for her Collection expanded with the first ever Children's Book Festival at the University of Southern Mississippi. Many of the letters she received in 1968 thank de Grummond for her invitation to the festival, and even though many to whom she reached out did not attend, they sent a contribution to the Collection. Her invitation to the conference was a clever way to introduce the Collection to many who had never heard of it before, and those who did attend were exceedingly impressed by the conference itself and the hospitality of the university. Margaret Ohler Hill, an author from Laramie, Wyoming, in a letter written shortly after the conference, raved about her experience:

June 8, 1968

Dear Dr. de Grummond,

Just a note to let you know what a stimulating experience the Hattiesburg conference was. I came home and wrote an article right away and got to work on my book. . . . I can't tell you how proud I am to be included in your author collections. Makes me resolve to be a more deserving author.

I love Hattiesburg and its warm, friendly people. It was especially wonderful meeting you. I do think you are such a splendid person, and so does everyone I talked to about you. . . .

In short, I think you did a beautiful job with the conference, and especially considering that this was its first year.

Thanks for inviting me!

Cordially,

Margaret

Adelaide Holl, an editor from New York City, echoed Margaret Ohler Hill's remarks, writing to "Lena" that "I'm still telling friends in New York how friendly and hospitable people in the South were to me. I do hope that if my schedule permits, I can come back to see you at your conference next year" (10 June 1968). She also adds in her last paragraph that "I have sent a letter to all our Carousel authors and artists telling them about your library collection and asking them to contribute materials they have to you. I hope they can add to your fine library." And they did, with Carousel author Mary Louise Foley sending de Grummond drafts of her book *The Caper Club Story* only a few weeks later. De Grummond truly served as a wonderful ambassador for Mississippi with this conference when political events at the time did not shine a positive light on the state.

The conference at the University of Southern Mississippi has become an annual rite of spring. The second year of the conference, de Grummond began awarding a specially "designed sterling silver medallion to an author or artist who has made an outstanding contribution to children's literature." The first recipient of this medallion was Lois Lenski, winner of the Newbery Medal in 1946 for *Strawberry Girl*, and author and illustrator of nearly one hundred books, half of which have been translated into fourteen languages. Newspaper accounts of the conference report that the award ceremony "drew an estimated crowd of 600 persons from Florida, Louisiana, Tennessee, and ten other states. It featured such distinguished names in this special literary field as author Joseph Krumgold, two-time winner of the John Newberry [sic] award and internationally known illustrator and writer Taro Yashima" ("First USM" n.p.).

De Grummond may have had a "Midas touch," but perhaps the better comparison is to *The Little Engine That Could*, due to her hard work and determination, which persisted throughout 1969 until her second mandatory retirement in 1970, and beyond. Of course, the word "retirement" meant nothing to de Grummond, and she continued to write letters, recruit authors and illustrators for the conference, and travel the world on behalf of the Collection. In 1970, the year of her second retirement, she had recently returned from Sussex, England, where she had presented the annual conference medallion to Mr. E. H. Shepard, illustrator of, most famously, *Winnie-the-Pooh* and *The Wind in the Willows*, because he was too ill to travel to Hattiesburg to accept it in person. De Grummond returned to Mississippi to discover that the children's literature collection she had established at the University of Southern Mississippi would, henceforth, be officially known as the "Lena Y. de Grummond Collection." De Grummond concludes her essay "Growth of an Idea" with this final thought after hearing the wonderful news: "Certainly retirement has not been an ending, but a beginning—and a very blessed one!" (6).

An undated photograph of Lena de Grummond. Courtesy of the de Grummond Collection.

THE LEGACY CONTINUES

Dee Jones

When I first became affiliated with the de Grummond Collection in 1975, it was well established under the diligent leadership of Dr. Lena Young de Grummond, its founder, and Elizabeth Perry, the librarian who oversaw day-to-day functions. I did not officially join the de Grummond Collection staff until 1980, although I contributed to the efforts of the Children's Book Festival by creating displays of original materials. My first appointment was as assistant to the curator in 1980, then assistant curator in 1981, and finally, curator in 1988.

From the start, my main responsibility and interest was to increase the accessibility and knowledge of the wealth of original materials and books tucked away on the fourth floor of McCain Library and Archives. Thousands of books were finally cataloged, with records added to the national Online Computer Library Center (OCLC) database. Dr. de Grummond had already done an amazing job of soliciting the donation of original artwork, manuscripts, and related books from hundreds of the best-known and loved authors and illustrators of children's literature. The Collection was already rich in original illustrations created by Randolph Caldecott, Kate Greenaway, and Walter Crane, as well as more than a hundred editions of Aesop's Fables in a number of different languages. Preceding me as curator was John Kelly, whose focus on collection development added many of the seminal British and American imprints of the eighteenth and nineteenth centuries, including those of publishers John Newbery, John Marshall, and the American Sunday-School Union.

When I became curator, I continued my quest to make the collection holdings more accessible, as well as building the book collection. Thanks to the hard work of Dr. Onva K. Boshears, Dr. Martin Pope, and Dr. Lillie Pope, the Ezra Jack Keats Collection was added by the early 1990s. With the assistance of Lay Lee Ong, the bulk of the extensive archive of H. A. and Margret Rey followed after Margret's death in 1996. There are only so many hours in a day, and it soon became obvious that more help was needed to catalog and process the newest acquisitions. We turned to the National Endowment for the Humanities for assistance and were successful in obtaining three major grants from 1990 through 2003, totaling $580,000, which enabled us to hire additional staff to process hundreds of collections of original manuscripts and illustrations and to create detailed finding aids. The rise of the internet in the mid-1990s allowed us to easily share this information with scholars throughout the world. The first iteration of the Collection's website went live in 1996 with technical assistance from graduate practicum student Sean George. The de Grummond Collection was finally on the digital map!

During my tenure as curator, I was assisted by remarkable colleagues including Ann Ashmore, Mary Hamilton, and Anne Lundin. Financial and moral support was provided by university presidents Dr. William D. McCain and Dr. Aubrey K. Lucas, as well as the dean of the libraries, Dr. Onva K. Boshears.

Additional national and international exposure of the Collection came with my committee memberships, presentations, lectures, and publications for professional organizations like the American Library Association (ALA), the Rare Books and Manuscripts section of ALA (RBMS), United States Board on Books for Young People (USBBY), the Society of Children's Book Writers and Illustrators (SCBWI), and the International Federation of Library Associations (IFLA). I was the first Mississippian to serve as a member of the American Library Association's Caldecott Committee in 2001. Exhibitions of original artwork from the de Grummond Collection holdings traveled to Japan on four separate occasions and also to Boston, Atlanta, New York, and Kansas.

Spreading the word about the de Grummond Collection gave me the opportunity to give talks throughout the United States and other countries including France, Ireland, Scotland, England, Canada, China, and Japan. A number of new programs that also increased awareness of the Collection included the Holiday Book Fair begun in 1986, the Ezra Jack Keats/de Grummond Collection Travel Fellowship begun in 1990, and the Curators and Catalogers Listserv begun in 1998. The Collection served as the host institution for the 1991 meeting of the Children's Literature Association, and on several occasions hosted groups of curators from other children's literature collections. Awards and recognitions include the *Library Journal netConnect* award for the Collection's website, the Leab American Book Prices Current Exhibition Catalogue Award for the "Curious George Comes to Hattiesburg" exhibition catalog, and a seat on the Mazza Gallery Board of Directors from 1998 to 2003.

I couldn't have asked for a more rewarding, fulfilling, and exciting way to spend twenty-four years of my professional life. Having recently celebrated its golden anniversary, the de Grummond Collection continues to grow in size and stature. Dr. de Grummond's dream is now in the hands of current and future curators who will bring their own distinctive style for years to come.

Chapter 2

Fables, Fairy Tales, and Folk Tales

Ruth B. Bottigheimer

Fables, short pithy stories meant to instruct readers in worldly wisdom, existed as exemplary literature for adults and children centuries before the genre became the world's first dedicated literature for children. Fairy tales, longer and more detailed stories, are usually meant to entertain and use magic to help heroes or heroines marry royalty, leave poverty behind, enjoy wealth and privilege, and live happily ever after. When fairy tales were first published in the 1550s, they were aimed at adult readers. Only in the 1700s did published fairy tales begin to be prepared specifically for child readers.

Fables in the modern world have a simple structure. Designed to exemplify a truth about human behavior (such as jealousy or acquisitiveness) or history (such as the habitual emergence of strong arbitrary political leaders), fables are closely related to proverbs. Their minimalist plots have a beginning, such as "There was once a dog in a manger," and proceed quickly to a conclusion, such as "Even though the dog couldn't eat the hay himself, he wouldn't let the cows near it" (the beginning and ending of one of Aesop's fables, "The Dog in the Manger," which illustrates selfishness). Largely dispensing with plot development, fables use animal characters to enact what is presented as natural facts of human behavior.

Title page of a 1549 edition of Aesop's fables in Greek and Latin. Courtesy of the de Grummond Collection.

As "exemplary stories," fables were prominent for over two thousand years. Those associated with Aesop, widely regarded as the genre's founder, are believed to date from the sixth or early fifth century BCE. No single fable can be directly attached to Aesop as author, yet his name is associated with an enormous body of literature, such as "The Fox and the Grapes." In this tale, a fox lusts after luscious grapes hanging just out of reach, but when he fails to reach them, he dismisses them as worthless. Fables were collected or composed by many in the ancient world, subsequently published in Latin and disseminated throughout Europe in the early and high middle ages.

A collection of equally lasting significance was the Indian *Panchatantra*. Translated from Sanskrit first into Persian, and in the seventh century CE from Persian into Arabic, the *Panchatantra* served as a source for re-workings that spread through the Muslim and Christian communities of Asia and Africa, eventually reaching Muslim Spain and from there across Europe as a whole. Tales in the *Panchatantra* and in *Kalila and Dimna*, a derivative Arabic collection, were organized into groups of related stories that were told within a framing tale about telling stories to achieve a goal, such as educating a prince or postponing an execution. Although individual fables remained both brief and simple, the overall frame tale within which they were presented was intriguing and sophisticated. Of all the *Panchatantra* stories, the best known perhaps concerns a frog who accepts a crocodile's invitation to carry him across a snake-infested river, with predictable results: the crocodile eats him during the crossing.

In the ancient world, fables were considered literature for adults, although the *Panchatantra* presented its fables as a painless form of educating a previously ineducable young prince. The early Indian collection prefigured the genre's entry into children's literature, where it remains, now intended largely for the very young. The de Grummond Collection's earliest set of fables is a 1530 edition of Aesop in Greek and Latin, while a contemporary collection of animal fables, *Feathers and Tails* (1992), draws from both Aesop and the *Panchatantra*.

Fairy tales emerged as popular stories in 1550s Venice, where they began to compete with, and eventually to displace, medieval romances among humble readers. Those had often ended with everlasting happiness achieved only after death or with renunciation of earthly bliss. In stark contrast, fairy tales offered happy endings here on earth. Giovan Francesco Straparola (c. 1485–c. 1557) crafted this newly secular happy ending in several tales in his *Le Piacevoli Notti* (1551, 1553; *The Pleasant Nights*). More significantly, he added poor girls and boys as possible heroes and heroines to the traditional roster of royal characters. In establishing the fairy tale genre, Straparola created the original plot for "Puss in Boots" in his "Costantino Fortunato." When his mother dies, Costantino, the youngest of three poor brothers, inherits only a cat. She, however, has magic powers (Straparola describes her as *fatata*) and soon gains the king's friendship and then the king's daughter for Costantino. By further cleverness she installs Costantino in a castle, where he lives happily ever after with his wife and children. Straparola also composed the first "Donkeyskin" (his "Tebaldo"), in which a princess flees her royal father's incestuous desire for her and finds eventual happiness as queen in a foreign land.[1] The de Grummond Collection holds the first complete translation of Straparola's tales into English, first published in London in 1894 and translated by W. G. Waters, titled *The Facetious Tales of Straparola* (1898).

Giambattista Basile of Naples (c. 1585–1632), a peripatetic courtier, injected a host of now-classic fairy tale motifs into his *Lo Cunto de li cunti* (1634–1636, *The Tale of the Tales*), enriching the genre with insertions from Ovid's retellings of Greek myths, *The Metamorphoses*, which was still a familiar school text in Basile's boyhood. This high classic material's presence amid the often low humor of his tales probably drew laughter from early listeners.

Straparola's and Basile's books with their fairy tales circulated in Paris in the 1690s, where Charles Perrault (1628–1703) reworked Straparola's "Costantino Fortunato" and "Tebaldo" respectively into "Le Chat botté" ("Puss in Boots") and "Peau d'Asne" ("Donkeyskin"). In addition, Perrault reworked Basile's "Sun, Moon, and Talia," "The Cat Cinderella," and "Three Fairies" into his "Belle au bois dormant" ("Beauty in the Sleeping Woods"), "Cendrillon" ("Cinderella"), and "Les Fées" ("The Fairies, or Diamonds and Toads"). He also borrowed elements from Basile's "L'Orsa" ("The She-Bear") for his "Donkeyskin" in his 1697 *Histoires, ou Contes du temps passé* (*Stories, or Tales of Past Time*).

Illustration captioned "Princess Doralice Hiding in the King's Chest," from *The Facetious Tales of Straparola*, from the first English translation in 1898, illustrated by Jules Garnier and E. R. Hughes (1898). Courtesy of the de Grummond Collection.

Perrault's tales were translated into English in 1729 and were subsequently edited into publications specifically for children, but they did not sell well, until they were adopted piecemeal by John Newbery nearly four decades later, and more successfully by his successors in children's book publishing at the end of the eighteenth century. The de Grummond Collection has rich and varied holdings of Perrault's tales, including a 1796 chapbook version of his "Sleeping Beauty" and an extensive collection of beautifully illustrated editions published by McLoughlin Brothers in New York between 1870 and 1920.

Hard on the heels of Perrault's publication of brief fairy tales in 1697, women like Marie-Jeanne Lhéritier (1664?–1734), Marie-Catherine d'Aulnoy (1651–1705), and Henriette-Julie de Murat (1670–1715) published collections that also included their reworkings of tales from Straparola's collection, but in longer and more detailed versions. Mme d'Aulnoy's work remained widely read in printings edited (in English) specifically for different female readerships: aristocratic, merchant, and artisan—entering the world of children's books in the 1750s. Contrary to general belief, it was the elaborate style of Mme d'Aulnoy's lengthy and complicated fairyland fictions that carried the day in the 1700s in English-speaking lands, rather than the now-iconic Perrault tales. The de Grummond Collection holds the first English edition of d'Aulnoy's *Tales of the Fairies*, printed by John Nicholson in London in 1707. In the 1750s, Jeanne-Marie Leprince de Beaumont (1711–1780) rewrote "Beauty and the Beast" for girl readers and presented it along with Bible stories and other fairy tales in a book translated into one European language after another, becoming one of the most far-reaching and influential early children's books.

In the Enlightenment-dominated world of early eighteenth-century English children's books, fairy tales were slow to take hold, but the London children's book publisher John Newbery (1713–1767) introduced them in the last years of his life. In the nineteenth century, fairy tales joined English-language children's literature from other countries. These included fairy and folk tales by Jacob (1785–1863) and Wilhelm (1786–1859) Grimm, Ludwig Bechstein (1801–1860), Hans Christian Andersen (1805–1875), and the international collections translated and edited by Andrew Lang (1844–1912) (and his wife) and Joseph Jacobs (1854–1916).

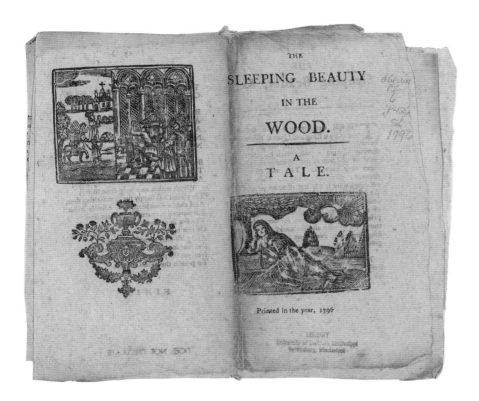

The de Grummond Collection holds many of these important fairy tale collections, including one of the very first English editions of Andersen, translated by Caroline Peachey and published in 1846, as well as a first edition of Jacobs's *English Fairy Tales* from 1890.

"Fairy stories," highly developed in nineteenth-century and early twentieth-century England, differ from "fairy tales." Beautifully illustrated with often tiny gauzy figures among garden or woodland flowers, fairy stories detail the lives and actions of "the little folk" in books for children. Some of the stories in Lang's *Red Fairy Book* (1890) qualify as fairy stories.

Another fairy-tale-related genre emerged in the later twentieth century when a wave of rewritten traditional fairy tales for young adult readers began to appear. They remain an important component of twenty-first-century children's literature. Jane Yolen's young adult (YA) novel *Briar Rose* (1992), for example, retells the Sleeping Beauty story in the context of

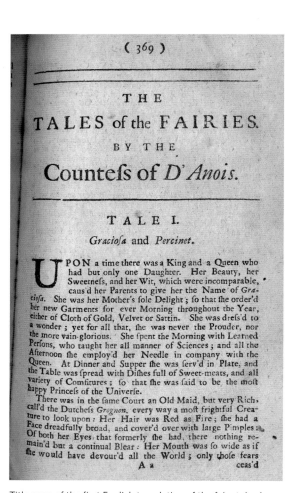

(369)

THE
TALES of the FAIRIES.
BY THE
Countefs of *D'Anois.*

TALE I.

Graciofa and *Percinet.*

UPON a time there was a King and a Queen who had but only one Daughter. Her Beauty, her Sweetnefs, and her Wit, which were incomparable, caus'd her Parents to give her the Name of *Graciofa*. She was her Mother's fole Delight ; fo that fhe order'd her new Garments for ever Morning throughout the Year, either of Cloth of Gold, Velvet or Sattin. She was drefs'd to a wonder ; yet for all that, fhe was never the Prouder, nor the more vain-glorious. She fpent the Morning with Learned Perfons, who taught her all manner of Sciences ; and all the Afternoon fhe employ'd her Needle in company with the Queen. At Dinner and Supper fhe was ferv'd in Plate, and the Table was fpread with Difhes full of Sweet-meats, and all variety of Comfitures ; fo that fhe was faid to be the moft happy Princefs of the Univerfe.

There was in the fame Court an Old Maid, but very Rich, call'd the Dutchefs *Grognon*, every way a moft frightful Creature to look upon : Her Hair was Red as Fire ; fhe had a Face dreadfully broad, and cover'd over with large Pimples : Of both her Eyes, that formerly fhe had, there nothing remain'd but a continual Blear : Her Mouth was fo wide as if fhe would have devour'd all the World ; only thofe fears
A a   ceas'd

Title page of the first English translation of the fairy tales by the Countess d'Anois (1707). Courtesy of the de Grummond Collection.

the Holocaust, while Malinda Lo's *Ash* (2009), a fantasy novel, retells the Cinderella story.

Folk tales differ fundamentally from fairy tales, and those differences are recognized by the way in which the Aarne-Thompson-Uther *Types of International Folktale: A Classification and Bibliography* is organized: "tales of magic" are numbered from 300 to 745; folk tales are scattered through separate listings for religious tales, realistic tales, animal tales, tales of the stupid ogre, anecdotes, jokes, and formula tales. Folk tales often end unhappily, with poor boys and girls, men and women, returning to poverty at the end. In contrast, happy-ever-after endings and an association with achieving happiness by means of a wedding remain closely associated with fairy tales. Nonetheless, terminologies often confuse the issue, with some authors (inaccurately) calling all the tales in the Grimm collection "fairy tales," while others call all of those tales, including fairy tales, "folktales."

Scholars are still arguing about whether fairy tales originated with and were spread by illiterate country people or were first composed by skilled writers like Straparola, Basile, and their literary descendants. New in the last thirty years are book-history-based studies that utilize the (newly discovered) presence of fairy tales in nineteenth-century elementary school textbooks, as well as in cheap pamphlets, colorful posters, and widespread newspapers as evidence to demonstrate print pathways for large-scale distribution of identical tellings of a core body of fairy and folk tales.[2] Studies of private and public reading practices in the nineteenth century add to the sense that printed fairy tales played a huge role in acquainting nineteenth-century city and country dwellers with traditional fairy tales.[3]

Notes

1. "Donkeyskin," widely believed to be a more ancient form of "Cinderella," is classified as such in the Aarne-Thompson-Uther *Tale Type Index.*

2. Ingrid Tomkowiak initiated the exploration of school books as sources of fairy and folk tale knowledge for children. Ruth B. Bottigheimer and Caroline Sumpter have written about other avenues of fairy tale distribution. Fairy tale posters are ubiquitous in library and rare book holdings, especially in Germany.

3. Rudolph Schenda described and analyzed public and private readings in the eighteenth and nineteenth centuries that acquainted city and country dwellers alike with fairy tales.

30   RUTH B. BOTTIGHEIMER

Hornbooks, Battledores, and Chapbooks

Laura E. Wasowicz

Hornbooks, battledores, and chapbooks refer to types of reading material for young children beginning to develop literacy skills, and all three are defined by a fairly specific physical format. The hornbook was among the earliest literacy tools produced for children between 1400 and 1800 CE. It consists of a single sheet of paper that usually contains an alphabet in upper and lowercase letters, followed by the numerals 1–9, 0 and (if there was room) basic prayers such as the Sign of the Cross, the Lord's Prayer, and the Hail Mary. The sheet of text (either handwritten or printed after the advent of moveable type in the 1450s) was laid on a paddle frame that could be anywhere between four and nine inches tall. The paper was covered with a protective transparent sheet of cow, goat, or sheep horn (made pliable by boiling), and the horn and paper were nailed to the paddle—lending the object its name. The horn sheet essentially protected the paper, which was a valuable commodity, especially before the mass production of paper became possible in the late eighteenth century. Hornbooks frequently had a hole drilled near the tip of the handle so they could be easily hung on a wall or attached by a strap to children's clothing for safekeeping. Although the types of material used to make hornbooks diversified over time to include ivory or metal that could be cast, etched, or painted with the educational text, the name stuck.

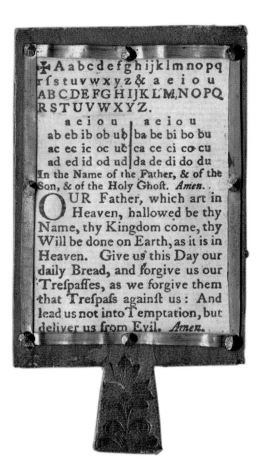

Eighteenth-century American hornbook. Courtesy of the de Grummond Collection.

The accompanying image from the de Grummond Collection exemplifies many features commonly identified with hornbooks, including the sturdy wooden paddle frame to which is nailed the single sheet of paper covered with a protective transparent sheet. A child's earliest reading exercises are distilled onto the neatly but densely printed sheet, starting with the lowercase and uppercase alphabets, followed by the vowels, a syllabary in which vowels are combined with the consonants b, c, and d in different configurations, and finally consummating in whole words expressing the Sign of the Cross and the full sentences constituting the Lord's Prayer.

The manufacture and use of hornbooks steadily declined in the latter half of the eighteenth century. Hornbooks were essentially replaced by cheaply produced paper books featuring multiple pages, a direct result of technological developments in the transatlantic world that made the economical production of paper on a massive scale possible. As members of a dying breed, many hornbooks were literally destroyed by generations of hard use at the hands of eager young readers. For this reason, today's extant hornbooks are precious survivors, underscoring the important role of special collections of historical children's literature like the de Grummond in preserving these early artifacts of children's print culture.

The battledore (also spelled battledoor) is the successor to the hornbook; originally, it contained a sheet of horned paper attached to a wooden rounded shuttlecock paddle. In the latter half of the eighteenth century, British publishers, including John Newbery and Benjamin Collins, issued battledores with a stiff paper cover. The paper battledore generally consists of two leaves of paper attached to a stiff paper outer wrapper. A distinctive flap with slanted edges attaches to the front cover, and the inner side of the flap has a piece of paper cut in the same trapezoid shape printed with the title, place of publication, publisher, and (if one is quite lucky) the date. The text frequently consists of an uppercase letter alphabet or a picture alphabet. If a battledore is viewed unfolded and the flap side is on the bottom, it resembles a shuttlecock racket without a handle. Battledores provided more flexibility than hornbooks because they could not only offer at least two pages of text, but the wrappers could be printed with additional text such as vowels and woodcut illustrations that were inexpensive to produce. Battledores were issued by American children's book

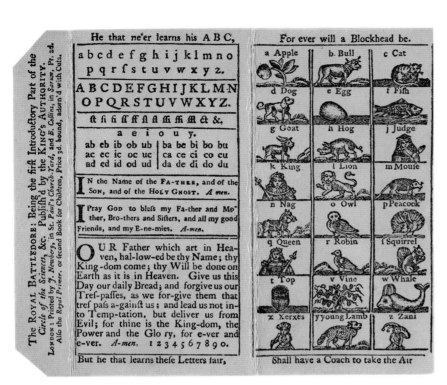

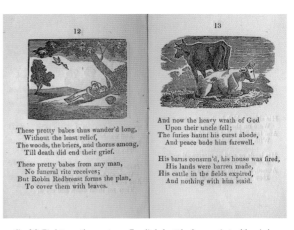

(Left) Eighteenth-century English battledore printed by John Newbery. Courtesy of the de Grummond Collection.

(Right) Page from *The Interesting Story of the Children in the Wood* (circa 1820), printed by J. G. Rusher. Courtesy of the de Grummond Collection.

publishers including Jacob Johnson (Philadelphia) and Samuel Wood (New York) in the first quarter of the nineteenth century, and then the format died out; however, in England the format survived until about 1860. It could be that American publishers might have felt less bound to the traditional quasi-hornbook shape of the battledore than English publishers, and the irregular shape of the oblong tab might have posed a logistical challenge that American printers did not find profitable to tackle. Battledores were essentially replaced by the increasingly popular chapbook, which first appeared in the seventeenth century.

The chapbook is a small rectangular shaped book, generally up to twelve centimeters (about 4½ inches) tall and eight to thirty-two pages long; chapbooks were frequently issued without bindings or in cheap paper wrappers. The term apparently refers to the term "chap man," a traveling peddler who would sell inexpensive goods. Chapbooks started to emerge in the seventeenth century as a cheap and portable means of

1884.] **APRIL.** [30 Days.

TAURUS ♉ *The Bull.*

1 Tu	All Fools' Day.	16 W	Shakespeare born, 1563.
2 W	Richard Cobden d., 1865.	17 Th	Benj. Franklin d., 1790.
3 Th	Tower opened free, 1873.	18 F	Liebig died, 1873.
4 F	Oliver Goldsmith d., 1774.	19 S	Lord Byron died, 1824.
5 S	Raikes died, 1811.	20 S	*Low Sunday.*
6 S	*Palm Sunday.*	21 M	Duke of Sussex d., 1843.
7 M	Prince Leopold b., 1853.	22 Tu	Wordsworth died, 1850.
8 Tu	Dr. Gale died, 1702.	23 W	St. George.
9 W	Lord Bacon died, 1626.	24 Th	Daniel de Foe died, 1731.
10 Th	Battle of Toulouse, 1814.	25 F	Princess Alice born, 1843.
11 F	Good Friday.	26 S	Jeremy Collier d., 1726.
12 S	Rodney's Victory, 1782.	27 S	*2nd Sunday after Easter.*
13 S	*Easter Sunday.*	28 M	Chaucer died, 1400.
14 M	Bank Holiday.	29 Tu	Russian War ended, 1856.
15 Tu	President Lincoln d., 1865.	30 W	Montgomery died, 1854.

☽ d. 2 h. 9 m. 17 A. ○ d. 10 h. 11 m. 44 M. ☾ d. 18 h. 3 m. 55 A. ● d. 25 h. 2 m. 58 M.

Page from Kate Greenaway's *Almanack for 1884* (1883).
Courtesy of the de Grummond Collection.

conveying popular literature, such as ballads that were initially printed on single sheet (and less portable), called a broadside; *The Children in the Wood* is a notable example of this migration across media. First published in broadside format as *The Norfolk Gentleman's Tragedy* in 1595 in England, the story of the unfortunate children in the wood was transformed from a ballad to a prose story for children; in 1796 Hartford, Connecticut, publisher John Babcock issued a chapbook version of *The Children in the Wood* "embellished with cuts."[1]

The chapbook format was also used to print the adaptations for children of novels like *Robinson Crusoe*. Many early chapbooks contained bawdy texts not necessarily meant for children. Publishers working in the emerging children's book market in the mid-eighteenth century used the format to print titles aimed squarely at the young because it was cheap to produce in large numbers. By the beginning of the nineteenth century, the chapbook format was appropriated by the rising number of religious tract societies both in Great Britain and the United States, like the London Tract Society and the American Sunday-School Union, to publish religious devotional material, Bible stories, and didactic fiction, much of it aimed at children and youth. The chapbook would survive as a popular format well into the twentieth century. One good example of a later pictorial chapbook in the de Grummond Collection is Kate Greenaway's *Almanack for 1926* issued by Frederick Warne in 1925; at eleven centimeters tall and twenty-four pages, it embodies the time-honored small format while featuring the artwork of one of the foremost illustrators of children's books.

Note

1. For a fleshed-out example of children's poetry migrating across media, cf. Patricia Crain's chapter on "The Literary Property of Childhood: The Case of the 'Babes in the Wood'" in her book *Reading Children: Literacy, Property and the Dilemmas of Childhood in Nineteenth-Century America* (University of Pennsylvania Press, 2016), pp. 43–61.

Chapter 4

READERS AND PRIMERS

Paige Gray

"Let us take a walk this fine day," opens the lesson entitled "The Cot-ton Field" [sic] in *The Southern Primer, Or, Child's First Lessons in Spelling and Reading* (1860). On this imaginary walk and pedagogical exercise, "We will go and see the field hands pick the snow from the white bolls" (27). The lesson goes on, instructing the child-reader to listen for the songs of said field hands and to take notice of their "nice huts" (27). Meanwhile, in the contemporaneous educational book *Sanders' Union Reader. Number One. For Primary Schools and Families* (1861), a lesson describes the fun to be had during playtime and states that "William" must "bring out the sword, the drum, and the flag" so he and the other boys can "march . . . soldiers round the play-ground" (63). These texts, part of the de Grummond Children's Literature Collection, reveal the ways in which materials created for white, privileged youth—even purposefully didactic and deceptively simple materials—illuminate cultural histories and how those cultures constructed ideas of childhood writ large. In the cases of the *Southern Primer* and the *Union Reader*, each work communicates values and ideals particular to either the child-reader living in a slave state or the child-reader residing above the Mason-Dixon Line in the years leading up to the outbreak of the American Civil War. Taken together, the de Grummond's holdings of readers and primers evidence the ideological power that comes both with and through the acquisition of language, particularly in regard to religious and national ideologies.

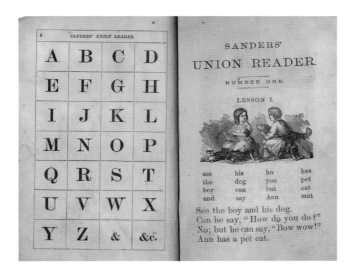

Indeed, as Jack Zipes, Lissa Paul, Lynne Vallone, Peter Hunt, and Gillian Avery explain, "In the Anglophone cultures, the links between literacy, power, and a Christian education are very deep" (77). These links become clear when examining historical readers and primers, those specific texts designed as a means to assist children in the acquisition of proficient language and literacy skills. Before the widespread use of printed readers and primers, children learned to read through paddle-shaped hornbooks, intended to help the young learn their letters and numbers, as well as religious tenets such as the Lord's Prayer. This relationship between literacy and Christianity in England and early America rendered the two nearly inextricable. In fact, "[t]he name *primer* initially only applied to prayer books used by the laity," Zipes, Paul, Vallone, Hunt, and Avery point out, "but because children learned to read from such books, the term came to mean any elementary book used to teach children to read" (78). While primers introduce basic literacy, readers provide collections of reading material that the beginner can use to practice and improve in skill.

One important early primer was *The New-England Primer*. "From the beginning of the eighteenth century, this little volume was a 'stock' item in the bookshops and village general stores of that region," writes Daniel Cohen, who relates that "untold thousands of copies were literally studied to pieces by children anxious (if not compelled) to learn to read" (52). The

(Left) Lesson 1 from the *Sanders' Union Reader* (1877). Courtesy of the de Grummond Collection.

(Right) The alphabet from an 1820 edition of the *New-England Primer*. Courtesy of the de Grummond Collection.

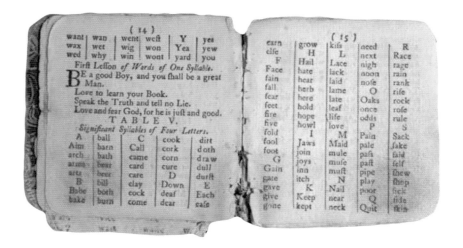

A lesson using words of one syllable from *The Royal Primer* (circa 1760). Courtesy of the de Grummond Collection.

de Grummond holds several early nineteenth-century editions of *The New-England Primer*, which claim to assist in the "more easy attaining" of "true reading of English" by way of alphabet and syllable instruction and through providing lists of common words organized by the number of syllables they contain. Each edition also includes catechisms and rhymes and opens with morning and bedtime prayers, ostensibly provided for the child-reader to memorize and recite, thus enabling the child to become more pious and dutiful. Rhymes published in *The New-England Primer* continue the Christian theme, with lines such as, "Though I am young a little one, / If I can speak and go alone, / Then I must learn to know the Lord, / And learn to read his holy word" (n. pag.).

The de Grummond also holds *The Royal Primer; or an Easy and Pleasant Guide to the Art of Reading*, printed in 1760 by "father of children's literature" John Newbery. In addition to the religious didacticism found in *The New-England Primer*, *The Royal Primer* subtlety conveys the virtues of loyal citizenship, equating service to the king with service to God. In addition to employing the common comparison of God and heaven to that of a monarch and his kingdom, *The Royal Primer* reminds readers that the text is "Authoriz'd by his Majesty King George II to be used throughout his majesty's dominion" (n. pag.). Here, "Authoriz'd" works to underscore the power that comes with literacy and authorship; King George "authorizes" through the vehicle of language.

The American readers contained in the de Grummond Children's Literature Collection provide a fascinating and telling history of children—and adults' ideas of children. Perhaps best known of these readers are the phonic-focused McGuffey Readers, which were first printed in 1836 and continued to be published and sold throughout the twentieth century, with nearly 125 million copies bought in the nineteenth century alone (Kammen 60). William Holmes McGuffey, (1800–1873) was a professor of Greek and Latin at Miami University of Ohio, where he began creating his iconic textbooks, and later served as the president of Cincinnati College. The six "grades" of McGuffey Readers indicate a progression of difficulty rather than suggesting what age or in which school grade a child should be to read a particular edition, thus helping teachers effectively "cope with students of differing ages and abilities" (Kammen 60). A student would be expected to recite lessons from the reader to prove mastery to the teacher for that particular McGuffey grade. For example, a lesson in the First Reader that many students likely recounted from memory for their teachers focuses on the different phonic uses of the vowel "e": "Ned has fed the hen. / She is a black hen. / She has left the nest. / See the eggs in the nest! / Will the hen let Ned get them?" (13). Rather than solely impart basic reading skills, these texts, like the earlier religious primers, seemingly served as a means to teach children *how* to be in the world. "The *Readers* embody strong moral lessons that children absorbed as they read their way through, lesson by lesson," argues Carol Kammen. She contends that this "was not accidental" being that the "purpose of nineteenth-century American schools—be it an old, established New England town school, an elite Southern school, or a frontier common school—was to prepare citizens in character and proper principles" (58).

In addition to texts seen as foundational to the American education system like the McGuffey Readers, the de Grummond also preserves educational tracts largely unknown, such as the *Southern Primer* and the *Union Reader*, as well as others including *My Very First Little Spanish Book* (1880) and *The Everlasting ABC and Primer* (1885). In *My Very First Little Spanish Book*, sentences written in Spanish (and translated into English) render scenes that stress the necessity and reward of youthful deference. Hence, the child-reader observes the dangers of straying too far from

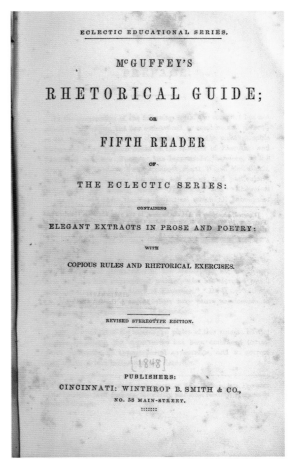

Title page from McGuffey's *Fifth Eclectic Reader* (1844). Courtesy of the de Grummond Collection.

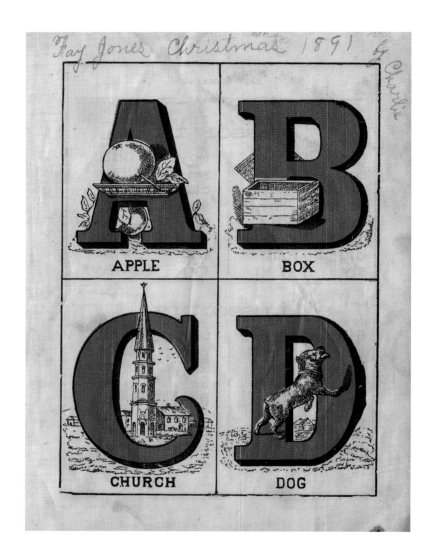

Page from *The Everlasting ABC and Primer* (1885). Courtesy of the de Grummond Collection.

home while also being shown the material rewards of heeding one's elders. *The Everlasting ABC and Primer*, meanwhile, highlights patriotic and religious duty through its choice of word and image to feature alongside each alphabetic letter, using a church for "C" and a soldier for "S," for instance. Within all, we see a morality for children built upon the development and improvement not only of language skills, but also obedience—be it to God, country, parent, or teacher.

Chapter 5

THE GOLDEN AGE OF ILLUSTRATED CHILDREN'S BOOKS

Alexandra Valint

Beginning in the mid-nineteenth century, the Golden Age of Children's Literature witnessed the rise of the beautiful, well-designed, artistic children's book that harmonized text and image. The increase in the aesthetic quality of illustrations in children's books was part of a larger trend; as Catherine Golden asserts, "[t]he Victorian illustrated book came into being, flourished, and evolved during the long nineteenth century" (2). Golden explains that in the first half of the century, caricature-style illustrations reigned, but starting in the 1860s, illustrations shifted towards a more realistic mode. George Cruikshank's illustrations for Charles Dickens's *Oliver Twist* (1837–39) and John Leech's illustrations for Dickens's *A Christmas Carol* (1843) are exemplary of this earlier period of drawing. Book illustration transformed over the century also due to developing technology that made the mass production of colored prints more efficient and affordable. Edmund Evans perfected a process of creating brilliantly pigmented illustrations; notably, he worked with the three most popular and influential children's book illustrators of the period: Walter Crane (1845–1915), Randolph Caldecott (1846–1886), and Kate Greenaway (1846–1901). The de Grummond's holdings are among the most significant collections of these three illustrators in North America.

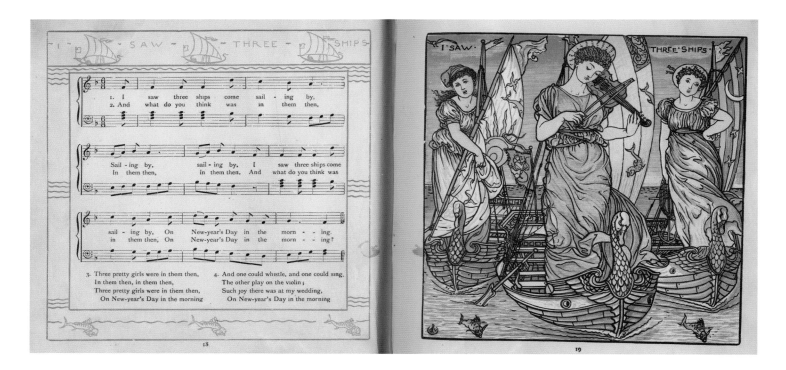

"I Saw Three Ships" from *The Baby's Opera* (1877) by Walter Crane. Courtesy of the de Grummond Collection.

Walter Crane believed his books could both educate and elevate the tastes of youthful readers. Each of his books maintains a unity of design from start to finish—including front and back covers, title pages, tables of content, dedication pages, and page borders. Crane utilizes the whole of each page; to use his own words, he approaches the page as "a space to be made beautiful in design" (*Of the Decorative* 17). One of his most famous works held in the de Grummond Collection, *The Baby's Opera* (1877) pairs illustrations with music and lyrics. The lyrics to "I saw three ships" simply mention "three pretty girls" in the approaching vessels. In Crane's illustration, these girls resemble the stunners of Pre-Raphaelite Brotherhood paintings in their colorful, flowing garb and voluptuous forms; their boats are detailed and lavishly decorated with scaly duck figureheads; each sail features a distinct astrological and nautical pattern. The borders of the music are fittingly ornamented with tiny ships and wavy lines. The specificity of the illustration goes beyond the lyrics' minimal information, yet everything on the page—illustration, border, lyrics—is

FORTVNE AND THE BOY

A Boy heedless slept by the well
By Dame Fortune awaked, truth to tell,
Said she "Hadst been drowned,
T would have surely been found
This by Fortune, not Folly befel."

FORTUNE · IS · NOT · ANSWERABLE · FOR · OUR · WANT · OF · FORESIGHT·

· 53 ·

"Fortune and the Boy" from *The Baby's Own Aesop* (1887) by
Walter Crane. Courtesy of the de Grummond Collection.

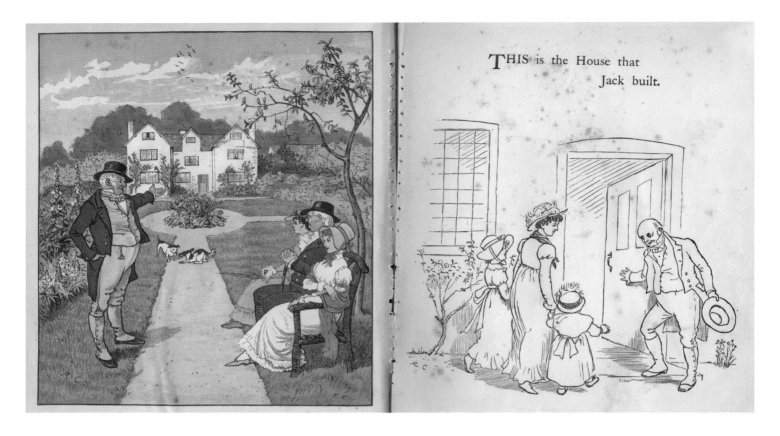

THIS is the House that
Jack built.

Page from *The House That Jack Built* (1878) by Randolph Caldecott. Courtesy of the de Grummond Collection.

connected thematically and visually. In *The Baby's Own Aesop* (1886), which presents brief summations of Aesop's fables, the collection's Greek inspiration is evident from the front cover of the de Grummond's 1887 edition. A toddler, in a tiny toga, knocks on a door situated between two Greek columns. (The c-shaped knocker and presence of two avian cranes are playful visual nods to Crane's authorship.) The title page includes Greek-styled vases and the Greek comedy and tragedy masks. Although the stories are focused on the foibles of animal characters, small details throughout—in clothing, architecture, interior decoration, and border design—continue the Greek theme.

Randolph Caldecott's illustrations are cherished for their sense of motion, liveliness, and good-natured humor. In contrast to Crane, he opted for less detail, famously telling his first biographer, Henry Blackburn, "the fewer the lines, the less error committed" (126). In both *The House That Jack Built* (1878) and *The Three Jovial Huntsmen* (1880), full-page color illustrations alternate with pen-and-ink sketch-like drawings. Maurice Sendak credits Caldecott's work for creating an innovative interplay of text and image: "Words are left out—but the picture says it. Pictures are left out—but the word says it. In short, it is the invention of the picture book" (21). For example, at one point in *The House That Jack Built*, the nursery rhyme indicates that a cat kills a rat. The subsequent two-page spread lacks words but first shows us how exactly the cat kills the rat (claws in its back!) and then reveals a dog spying on the unsuspecting cat; turn the page, and the text informs the reader that the cat ironically becomes the dog's victim. These wordless interludes flesh out the barebones rhyme while also propelling the story forward. In *The Three Jovial Huntsmen*, these two-page sections illustrate the trio of hunters from the side, from the front, from behind; we see their horses midleap, midstride, stopping for water; we see the group in close-up and at a great distance. The shifting perspectives create the impression of movement and speed; they convey the sheer joy of riding a horse through the countryside with one's friends, even if (maybe especially if) one doesn't find anything suitable to hunt.

While many of Caldecott's books immortalize a lively English countryside, Kate Greenaway's world is populated by flowers, gardens, and women and children clothed in a distinctive set of charmingly antiquated hats and dresses. *Under the Window* (1879), which couples illustrations with her own verses, was her first book and an immense critical and popular success. Greenaway's "juvenile Arcadia," Anne Lundin writes, "led to the phenomenal 'Greenaway Vogue' of ephemera, commercial products, and imitations of her highly original designs" (146). The book's opening lines, "Under the window is my garden, / Where sweet, sweet flowers grow," takes us through the portal of the window into an Eden of children's games and dances in which children and flowers are akin (Greenaway 15). In one illustration, five sisters wearing matching green coats adorn the top of the page and, mirror-like, five pots of green-stemmed marigolds line the base of the page. *The Pied Piper of Hamelin* (1888), Greenaway's illustrated version of the 1842 Robert Browning poem of the same name, possesses an earthy palette and medieval costumes unlike Greenaway's

Page from *The Pied Piper of Hamelin* by Robert Browning, illustrated by Kate Greenaway (1888). Courtesy of the de Grummond Collection.

typical fare. When a town refuses to pay the piper for successfully drawing out the rat population, the piper lures the town's children to a new land. Greenaway often depicts children dancing and playing in her works, and this investment manifests in the visual climax of her interpretation: she dedicates ten full pages to representing the children's joyous following of the piper even though Browning only spends eleven of his 303 lines on the scene. While Browning's poem ends on a somber, instructive note reiterating the town's guilt and loss, Greenaway's depiction of the children's destination suggests that they have not been stolen so much as liberated. In a return to a typical Greenaway scene and color scheme, the children don white dresses and floral laurels, and they frolic by the riverside on the green grass under a tree spouting pink blossoms; several children hug and rest on the piper, the only adult present. Although the piper promises this juvenile paradise to the children, it is not as definitively reached in Browning's poem as it is in Greenaway's illustration. Not only does the de Grummond contain these two popular titles and many others, but the Kate Greenaway Papers also include letters, sketches, unpublished manuscripts and drawings, woodblocks engraved by Evans, and even Greenaway's early-career greeting cards.

Many illustrators tackled the challenge of representing fantastical creatures and settings through realism. John Tenniel, a cartoonist for *Punch*, created the memorable illustrations for Lewis Carroll's *Alice's Adventures in Wonderland* (1865) that impressively "make Wonderland look believable" by employing "shading, crosshatching, and outlining to lend Alice photographic realism" (Golden 139). Beatrix Potter, most famous for her *Peter Rabbit* stories (first printed in 1901 and published in 1902), drew animals that looked realistic despite being clothed. She based many of her illustrated animals on her own pets, and her years of naturalistic study and sketching trained her to create such lifelike nature illustrations. Potter's anthropomorphized Peter—in his blue brass-buttoned jacket—and Tenniel's White Rabbit—in vest and jacket, armed with umbrella and pocket watch—both walk and dress like humans but also visually resemble real rabbits.

These British illustrators were popular on both sides of the Atlantic, particularly Greenaway, who was endlessly pirated and imitated. But according to Robert Lawson, Howard Pyle is responsible for issuing in "a Golden Age of American illustration" with his "vivid and understanding portrayals of the ragged heroes" (115, 122). In his pen-and-ink drawings for *The Merry Adventures of Robin Hood* (1883), the title character repeatedly stands tall and confident with a distinctive feather in his pointy hat. In *The Story of King Arthur and His Knights* (1903), Pyle's black-and-white illustrations dramatically render a mostly male world of strong knights, looming castles, and vigorous fighting—very unlike Greenaway's softer, feminine domain. Pyle also educated a whole generation of American illustrators, now known as the Brandywine School. His students included N. C. Wyeth, who illustrated Robert Louis Stevenson's *Treasure Island* (1911) and *Kidnapped* (1913) for Scribner's Illustrated Classics series. In 1937, however, librarians in the United States chose Caldecott to represent their children's illustration award; librarians in the United Kingdom chose Greenaway in 1955. Although modern children's book illustration remains indebted to these Golden Age illustrators and publishers, as Crane himself wrote, "pictured-books may be called the hand-glass which still more intimately reflects the life of different centuries and peoples" (*Of the Decorative* 14).

Mr. McGregor chases Peter in *The Tale of Peter Rabbit* (1904), written and illustrated by Beatrix Potter. Courtesy of the de Grummond Collection.

Chapter 6

Children's Series Fiction

Amy Pattee

Series fiction denotes two or more published narratives that tell the story of a character or group of characters in sequential or episodic form. Individual series may be progressive and describe the growth and development of one or more protagonists over time, or may be successive and depict the adventures or challenges faced by one or more protagonists who change very little from volume to volume. While a number of works of children's literature in series have been recognized for their literary excellence, series fiction for young people, as a whole, is a historically marginalized form. This literary marginalization is a byproduct of series fiction's historical association with the dime novel, its related association with commodity rather than art, and its common status as popular fiction.

With its inaugural volume published in 1835, Jacob Abbott's Rollo series (1835–1863) is considered by many to be among the first American children's literary series, most volumes of which are held by de Grummond. A progressive series describing the growth and adventures of a boy named Rollo, Abbott's novels reflect the didacticism common to children's literature of the early nineteenth century. The twenty-seven-volume series is composed of ten novels depicting Rollo's moral and intellectual development from ages five to eight; four novels of "Rollo's Philosophy," featuring short stories followed by questions meant to encourage scientific observation and reasoning; ten novels describing twelve-year-old Rollo's

"Grand Tour" of Europe; and three books of original and selected works of poetry ostensibly collected for Rollo and his cousin Lucy. Concurrent with the publication of the Rollo series, Abbott created the Cousin Lucy series (1841–1842) focusing on Rollo's younger female cousin. As the introductory paratext printed in the six Cousin Lucy novels noted the series' particular address to girls, the Rollo and Cousin Lucy series are among the first works of children's literature to explicitly distinguish their readers by gender.

Series fiction following Rollo, like Martha Finley's progressive Elsie Dinsmore series (1867–1905; an 1867 edition of the first novel in the series, *Elsie Dinsmore*, is held in the de Grummond Collection), retained Abbott's series' didacticism while participating in and helping to shape developing literary genres, like the domestic novel (e.g., Louisa May Alcott's *Little Women* [1868] and its sequels) and the adventure story (e.g., Oliver Optic's the Boat Club series [1855–1860]). In fact, some scholars and critics have positioned Finley's series as a children's literary lynchpin, pointing out its similarity to Susan Warner's best-selling *Wide, Wide World* (1850) (Avery 13; MacLeod 153) and suggesting that the character of Elsie established a literary template from which later series heroines, including Nancy Drew, were drawn (Johnson 13).

As Abbott's Rollo and Finley's Elsie Dinsmore novels were being published, popular periodical and dime novel publishing experienced significant growth. These popular writings expanded readers' literary horizons in the form of serialized tales (in periodicals) and series fiction (in both dime novels and periodicals) reflecting the budding genres of mystery (e.g., Street and Smith's Nick Carter Detective Library [1891–1896]), the Western (e.g., Frank Tousey's Wide Awake Library [1878–1896], in which the first story about Jesse James appeared), and, eventually, science fiction (e.g., Frank Tousey's Frank Reade Library [1892–1898]). Decried by some as subliterary, these popular publications, many of which are held in the de Grummond Collection, helped to establish not only the mass literary market for children and adults but also a model, market, and marketplace for series fiction.

Consequently, the turn of the twentieth century and its first two decades saw a dramatic increase in the number and diversity of series

ROLLO ON THE TREE BRIDGE.—Page 14.

Page from Jacob Abbott's *Rollo at Play* (1867). Courtesy of the de Grummond Collection.

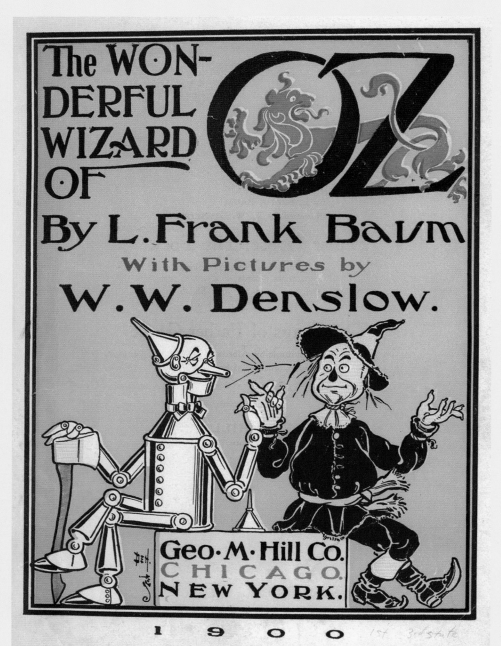

Title page of *The Wonderful Wizard of Oz* by L. Frank Baum, illustrated by W. W. Denslow (1900). Courtesy of the de Grummond Collection.

created for young people. Domestic series like Susan Coolidge's Katy series (1872–1890) and L. M. Montgomery's *Anne of Green Gables* (1908) and its sequels; fantasy tales like L. Frank Baum's Oz series (1900–1920); adventure series like the Camp Fire Girls (1910–1939); and the science fiction series Tom Swift (1910–1945, first series) are among the notable series published during this period available in whole or part in the de Grummond Collection.

The year 1905, when Edward Stratemeyer established his Stratemeyer Literary Syndicate, marks a turning point in the history of series fiction for youth. Stratemeyer, a prolific author of dime novels, established the Syndicate to mass produce fiction in series for young people. The Syndicate hired ghostwriters who were paid a fee to write individual books based on outlines Stratemeyer provided; these ghostwritten books were produced by publishers with whom the Syndicate had a relationship and shared a profit (for examples of this process, see the Andrew E. Svenson Papers archived at the de Grummond). While the most popular Syndicate series are the Nancy Drew Mystery Stories (1930–present) and the Hardy Boys (1927–present), the Syndicate was, by various accounts, ultimately responsible for more than one hundred series, many of which continued the tradition of "gendered" address established with the Rollo and Cousin Lucy series and were implicitly or explicitly pitched to boy or girl readers.

Syndicate-style literary production has challenged critics invested in biographical, New Critical, and Marxist approaches to literature to reconsider their definitions of literary art with regards to its creation. While these critics have compared mass market series production to the assembly line and suggested that this mode of production begets formulaic and largely plot-driven fiction that pays little attention to style and characterization, series fiction devotees—including readers and critics—have found and continue to find meaning and significance in these popular works.

Criticism aside, there is no doubt that Stratemeyer's production model strongly influenced series fiction publishing in the latter half of the twentieth century. The Syndicate arguably set the standard for contemporary book packaging and youth series production, paving the way for companies like 17th Street Productions (now Alloy Entertainment), the book packaging group responsible for the Sweet Valley High series (1983–2003);

The Camp Fire Girls
In The Woods

CHAPTER I

THE ESCAPE

"Now then, you, Bessie, quit your loafin' and get them dishes washed! An' then you can go out and chop me some wood for the kitchen fire!"

The voice was that of a slatternly woman of middle age, thin and complaining. She had come suddenly into the kitchen of the Hoover farmhouse and surprised Bessie King as the girl sat resting for a moment and reading.

Bessie jumped up alertly at the sound of the voice she knew so well, and started nervously toward the sink.

"Yes, ma'am," she said. "I was awful tired—an' I wanted to rest a few minutes."

"Tired!" scolded the woman. "Land knows *you* ain't got nothin' to carry on so about! Ain't you got a good home? Don't we board you and give you a good bed to sleep in? Didn't Paw Hoover give you a nickel for yourself only last week?"

3

Page from Jane Stewart's *The Camp Fire Girls in the Woods* (1914). Courtesy of the de Grummond Collection.

created for young people. Domestic series like Susan Coolidge's Katy series (1872–1890) and L. M. Montgomery's *Anne of Green Gables* (1908) and its sequels; fantasy tales like L. Frank Baum's Oz series (1900–1920); adventure series like the Camp Fire Girls (1910–1939); and the science fiction series Tom Swift (1910–1945, first series) are among the notable series published during this period available in whole or part in the de Grummond Collection.

The year 1905, when Edward Stratemeyer established his Stratemeyer Literary Syndicate, marks a turning point in the history of series fiction for youth. Stratemeyer, a prolific author of dime novels, established the Syndicate to mass produce fiction in series for young people. The Syndicate hired ghostwriters who were paid a fee to write individual books based on outlines Stratemeyer provided; these ghostwritten books were produced by publishers with whom the Syndicate had a relationship and shared a profit (for examples of this process, see the Andrew E. Svenson Papers archived at the de Grummond). While the most popular Syndicate series are the Nancy Drew Mystery Stories (1930–present) and the Hardy Boys (1927–present), the Syndicate was, by various accounts, ultimately responsible for more than one hundred series, many of which continued the tradition of "gendered" address established with the Rollo and Cousin Lucy series and were implicitly or explicitly pitched to boy or girl readers.

Syndicate-style literary production has challenged critics invested in biographical, New Critical, and Marxist approaches to literature to reconsider their definitions of literary art with regards to its creation. While these critics have compared mass market series production to the assembly line and suggested that this mode of production begets formulaic and largely plot-driven fiction that pays little attention to style and characterization, series fiction devotees—including readers and critics—have found and continue to find meaning and significance in these popular works.

Criticism aside, there is no doubt that Stratemeyer's production model strongly influenced series fiction publishing in the latter half of the twentieth century. The Syndicate arguably set the standard for contemporary book packaging and youth series production, paving the way for companies like 17th Street Productions (now Alloy Entertainment), the book packaging group responsible for the Sweet Valley High series (1983–2003);

and Pleasant Company (now American Girl, Inc.), the publishing, media, and doll-manufacturing company responsible for the American Girl series (1986–present).

The Syndicate novels and the series they influenced were primarily successive in form and, as such, were distinct from the first progressive series of the mid-nineteenth century. That many of these early books in series (e.g., *Little Women*, *Anne of Green Gables*) are now considered classics has likely contributed to the contemporary professional and critical preference for progressive rather than successive series. Unlike successive series, which often privilege plot over character development, modern and contemporary progressive series, like Laura Ingalls Wilder's Little House (1932–1943), Maud Hart Lovelace's Betsy-Tacy (1940–1955), Beverly Cleary's Ramona (1955–1999), Mildred D. Taylor's Logan Family (1975–2001), and Rita Williams-Garcia's Gaither Sisters (2010–2015), describe the growth and maturation of one or more child protagonists over multiple volumes, achieving the narrative goal many associate with and celebrate in children's literature.

Editions and Variants

Eric L. Tribunella

Classic children's books are published, republished, edited, abridged, and revised over time, with each new edition potentially introducing differences both small and large among the multiple versions. Differences among variants reflect developments or mistakes in printing and editing practices, the evolution of ideals or assumptions about children and childhood, and the alteration of texts for different uses, ages, or eras. One of the hallmarks of the de Grummond is its extensive collection of multiple editions of works, including, for example, more than fifty copies of *The Secret Garden* (1911), more than sixty of *Little Women* (1868), and more than a hundred of *Alice's Adventures in Wonderland* (1865). Examining differences among multiple editions and variants, many of which are now extremely rare, enables a textual study of children's literature that is only possible with large archival collections.

An "edition" of a work simply refers to "all copies of a book that are printed from one setting of type, whether directly from the type or indirectly through plates made from it" (Williams and Abbott 22). David Greetham asserts that "substantial sections of the entire text" must be reset to qualify as a new edition, so it follows that minor changes or corrections to the type can result in multiple variants of a single edition, in addition to variations among different editions (167). Sometimes changes to a text can be minor, such as the correction or modernization of spelling and punctuation. Other changes can be much more significant, such as the addition or deletion of words or sections, including prefaces or forewords, illustrations, or the larger portions of texts omitted from abridgements.

Johannes Amos Comenius's *Orbis Sensualium Pictus* illustrates the importance of variant editions to the history of children's literature. An illustrated German-Latin textbook, it was first published in 1653. Charles Hoole produced an English translation within a year of its initial publication, followed by multiple new editions that continued to be produced for more than a century. Comenius paired an image of a scene or object, like a feast or the human body, with a list of words in two languages corresponding to parts of the image. Its variant editions have been important to the history of children's literature by disseminating a model of how to use illustrations to facilitate instruction and engage readers, and critics sometimes trace the genealogy of picture books to *Orbis Pictus*. It also provides an index to evolving paradigms in children's education. The editor of the twelfth London edition from 1777 notes his insertion of a chapter on botany, "a study much in vogue," and another on Noah's flood, along with updates based on discoveries concerning the circulation of blood. The addition of a Biblical story alongside the emendation of modern scientific thought suggests a harmonious relationship between the natural and the spiritual worlds in the late eighteenth century. The de Grummond Collection's earliest copy of *Orbis Pictus* is a 1705 printing of Hoole's translation, which can be compared with another English edition from 1777, a German edition from 1838, and an American edition from 1968.

Some alterations can impact the meaning or reception of a work. For instance, Anne Hiebert Alton, in a 2001 edition of *Little Women*, documents changes Louisa May Alcott made between the 1868 and 1880 editions, including formalizing the speech and altering descriptions of characters. Beth's original statement that she "can't practise good a bit" becomes "can't practise well at all," making Beth seem more proper. Marmee goes from being "stout" and not "particularly handsome" to "tall" and "noble-looking," equating Marmee's moral stature with physical attractiveness (34). More recently, the 1988 edition of Hugh Lofting's *The Story of Doctor Dolittle*, a novel first published in 1920, omits troubling references to the race of characters and a chapter in which Dolittle helps an African prince turn

Page from a 1705 edition of Comenius's *Orbis Sensualium Pictus*, translated into English by Charles Hoole and printed by John Sprint. Courtesy of the de Grummond Collection.

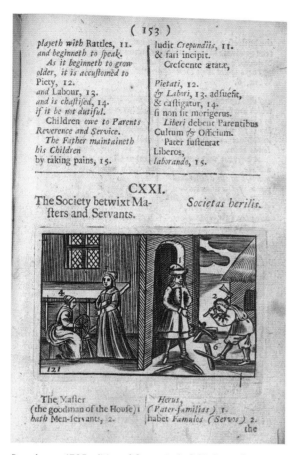

Page from a 1705 edition of Comenius's *Orbis Sensualium Pictus*, translated into English by Charles Hoole and printed by John Sprint. Courtesy of the de Grummond Collection.

white in order to woo a woman he believes is Sleeping Beauty. The sanitary belt Margaret uses in the first edition of Judy Blume's *Are You There God? It's Me, Margaret* from 1970 has been changed to a pad in recent versions, allowing the book to continue instructing newer generations without becoming outdated. First published in 1973, the picture book *black is brown is tan* features a poem by Arnold Adoff about an interracial family, with illustrations by Emily McCully. The 2002 edition includes all new illustrations by McCully that updates the family's personal and sartorial styles, along with some modifications to the poem, such as different line breaks.

Nonfiction in particular risks becoming dated, and tracking revisions to children's informational texts points to new discoveries or ways of thinking and how they are communicated to children. The 1973 edition of Herbert S. Zim's *The Universe* updates a chart from the original 1961 edition showing the measured brightness of stars in some of the constellations, indicating advances in astronomy, while the 1960 edition of W. Maxwell Reed's *The Earth for Sam* refers to "primates" rather than the racially charged "white primates," as the original 1930 edition had. Textual scholarship traces changes like these and considers their significance and meaning.

In 2007 the grandson of James Otis Kaler (1848–1912) made a donation to the de Grummond Collection that included more than a dozen editions of his grandfather's most famous work, *Toby Tyler; or, Ten Weeks with a Circus* (written under the pen name, James Otis), which helped popularize the narrative of the boy who runs away with the circus. The archive's copies range from an 1881 first edition to a 1990 reprint. The text of *Toby Tyler* changes in numerous, sometimes minute ways across editions. A 1971 edition edited by Grace Hogarth minimizes some of the gruesome details of the death of Toby's pet monkey. For instance, as the monkey dies from a gunshot wound in the original text, he looks up at Toby and places "one little brown paw to his breast, from which the blood was flowing freely" (247). The Hogarth edition drops the latter phrase and the description of Toby's getting covered in blood as he embraces his beloved companion. The original edition refers to Toby as a "very small boy," while Hogarth's omits "very small" from the description. Details such as these may seem minor, but their cumulative effect can change a reader's impressions or the

A variety of editions of Frances Hodgson Burnett's *The Secret Garden* in the de Grummond Collection. Photograph by Kelly Dunn.

"HOW I LOVE YOU, MR. STUBBS!"

Toby mourns his monkey. From James Otis's *Toby Tyler; or, Ten Weeks with a Circus* (1881). Courtesy of the de Grummond Collection.

text's meaning. These sample changes suggest a modern impulse to shield children from grisly descriptions of bloodshed and a more pronounced expectation that boyhood masculinity be signaled by physical virility. Access to multiple editions of a single work, like the Kaler Collection in the de Grummond, permits readers to trace changes to texts across time and to develop a fuller understanding of the history of children's literature.

Chapter 8

Nineteenth-Century Children's Magazines

Lorinda Cohoon

Periodicals for children flourished in the nineteenth-century publishing culture, and the de Grummond Collection contains many examples of nineteenth-century children's periodicals. The Collection also houses valuable reference material and scholarship on children's magazines. Digital repositories have made accessing nineteenth-century children's magazines easier, but hard copies of children's periodicals in bound annual volumes and in single issues often contain additional material such as advertisements, complete indexes, and handwritten marks of readership and ownership that cannot always be accessed in digital versions. Intersections between women's and gender studies, American studies, transatlantic studies, and studies of the material culture of the book and children's literature scholarship have drawn attention to the rich potential for studying children's magazines as spaces that offer publishing opportunities for writers who might otherwise be marginalized in other areas of literary culture.

For example, Nazera Sadiq Wright's essay "'Our Hope Is in the Rising Generation': Locating African American Children's Literature in the Children's Department of the *Colored American*," which appears in Anna Mae Duane and Katherine Capshaw's edited collection *Who Writes for Black Children? African American Children's Literature Before 1900*, usefully

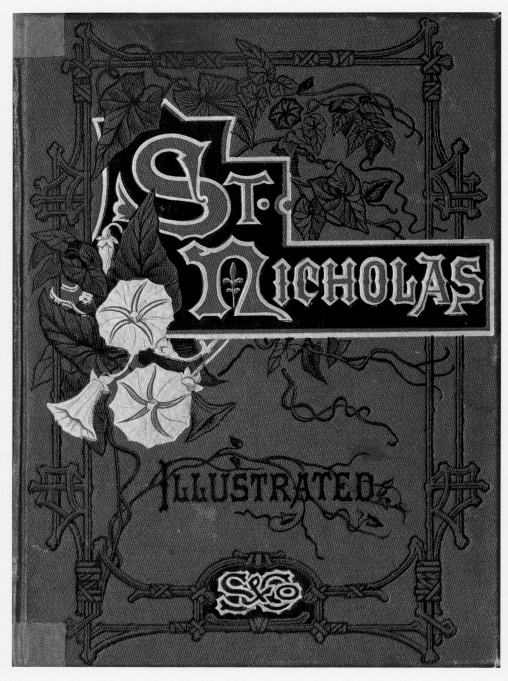

An issue of *St. Nicholas* magazine. Courtesy of the de Grummond Collection.

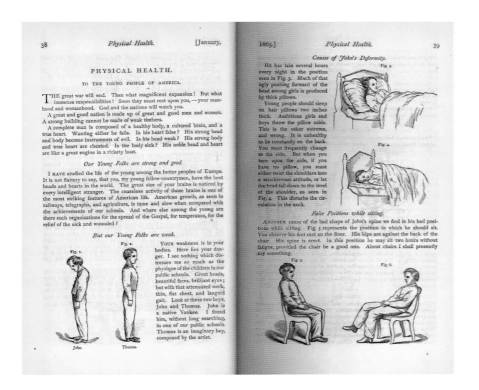

A lesson on physical health from the first issue of *Our Young Folks: An Illustrated Magazine for Boys and Girls* (1865). Courtesy of the de Grummond Collection.

examines how reprintings can be analyzed to think about the critiques and emphases that are inherently embedded in choosing to reprint and recirculate certain texts. Since the de Grummond houses many periodicals that are sources for reprintings in a variety of contexts and also periodicals that contain reprintings themselves, the archive provides valuable resources for exploring the possibilities for locating and understanding children's texts read by African American children before 1900. Comparison of reprinted pieces across nineteenth-century periodicals for children also offers information about bylines, pseudonyms, or anonymous publications that adds to understandings of both marginalized and celebrated texts and authors whose writings and topics are circulated and recirculated in periodical form.

Children's periodicals are repositories for key details about writing for children during the nineteenth century, and they contain layered and significant information about children's culture and texts offered to children.

Some periodicals and other resources related to children's periodicals housed in the archive include *Our Young Folks*, first published in 1871, and *St. Nicholas* magazine, first published in 1873, as well as magazines that begin in the late nineteenth century and run into the twentieth, such as Beeton's *Boy's Own Paper* running from 1832 to 1902. There are also copies of *Boys' Life* and *Girl's Own Paper*. Some lesser known magazines such as *The Great Round World and What Is Going On in It: A Weekly Newspaper for Boys and Girls* are also available in the de Grummond. Other key resources available for examination include *American Boy, Francis Forrester's Boys' and Girls' Magazine*, and *Fireside Companion* and *Student and Schoolmate*, the last of which is an offshoot of *Forrester's Boys' and Girls' Magazine*.

In addition to hard copies of periodicals, the de Grummond houses some papers and manuscripts related to *St. Nicholas* correspondence. Other papers, including the Cornelia Lynde Meigs Papers, contain manuscripts of short stories published in *St. Nicholas* magazine. Among papers and manuscripts housed in the archive, there are holdings that promise useful materials for scholarship on women's contributions to children's periodicals. For example, the Emilie Blackmore and Marie Graham Stapp Papers contain materials and manuscripts related to works published in children's magazines in the 1920s.

Online and microform editions of many children's periodicals are available as resources to supplement hard copies housed in the stacks of archives like the de Grummond. For example, *The Slave's Friend* is available online and can be put into conversation with the de Grummond's *Juvenile Miscellany*. While the de Grummond does not have a full run of *The Youth's Companion*, patrons will have access to online versions and be able to examine runs that start in 1879 and 1929. The de Grummond also has reference sources such as Richard Cutts's *Index to the Youth's Companion* as well as indexing notes on earlier volumes taken by former de Grummond curator and archivist Dee Jones.

There are other scholarly resources available in the de Grummond's holdings including studies of *St. Nicholas* magazine, such as Lisa Weil's 2007 thesis about advertising in *St. Nicholas*: "'A Good Line of Advertising': The Historical Development of Children's Advertising as Reflected

Part 169—February, 1894. *CONTAINING THE NUMBERS FOR JANUARY.* Price 6d.

Frontispiece:—THE WRECK.

Drawn by JOSEPH BELL.

The Illustrations in this part are drawn by Joseph Bell, Lucien Davies, Elmeric de St. Dalmas, Davidson Knowles, G. H. Edwards, Harrison Miller, A. J. Baker, H. Corrodi, Marcella Walker, A. T. Elwes, and others.

THE "LEISURE HOUR" OFFICE, 56, PATERNOSTER ROW, E.C.

Table of contents for the February 1894 issue of *The Girl's Own Paper*. Courtesy of the de Grummond Collection.

in *St. Nicholas Magazine* 1873–1905." Other resources include scholarship on race in children's magazines, including titles such as Brandy Parris's "Difficult Sympathy in the Reconstruction-Era Animal Stories of *Our Young Folks*." Other texts that examine the history of advertising in connection with children's literature and culture, such as Paul B. Ringel's *Commercializing Childhood: Children's Magazines, Urban Gentility, and the Ideal of the Child Consumer in the United States, 1823–1918* (2015) show the connections between nineteenth-century periodical literature and other areas of cultural and economic change.

Children's periodicals continue to provide rich, sometimes untapped, resources for scholars interested in the complexities of nineteenth-century children's literature and culture, and the de Grummond archive offers scholars a treasure trove of material related to children's periodicals that can and should be used to expand our understanding of this rich and varied form of children's literature.

Dolls, Toys, Toy Books, and Games

Megan Norcia

The study of children's material culture is a growing field, but by no means a new topic. John Newbery's *A Little Pretty Pocket-Book* (1744), often identified as a foundational text for establishing the children's specialty book market, was sold with a toy to appeal to child consumers. With the growth of children's literature as a field and the establishment of special collections since the 1970s, study of material culture has grown. The de Grummond Collection, including a fine 1787 American edition of Newbery's book, demonstrates that children's play objects are themselves rich texts that tell important stories. Children's playthings inspire their complex creative lives, and their toys and games remain as artifacts of a particular time and place, long after the children who played with them have grown. Even seemingly disposable toys like a *Charlotte's Web* toy plush spider expose our culture's marketing ploys, commodification of literature, kinesthetic learning applications, and manufacturing practices.

Children's literature enjoys a close relationship with toys: after Newbery, Mary Ann Kilner's *Adventures of a Pincushion* (c. 1780) and *Memoirs of a Peg-Top* (c. 1790) continue to demonstrate the eighteenth-century fascination with objects associated with daily life. From the late eighteenth

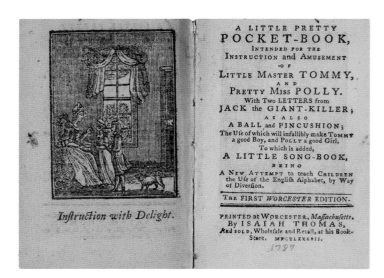

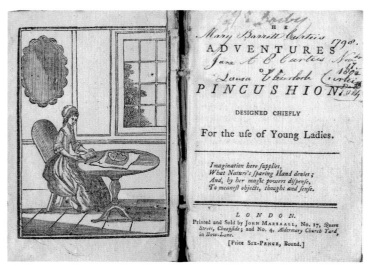

(Left) Title page of John Newbery's *A Little Pretty Pocket-Book*, printed by Isaiah Thomas (1787). Courtesy of the de Grummond Collection.

(Right) Title page of *The Adventures of a Pincushion, Designed Chiefly for the Use of Young Ladies* by Mary Ann Kilner (1791?). Printed and sold by John Marshall. Courtesy of the de Grummond Collection.

century onward, the toy industry mass-produced toy soldiers and dolls that inspired children like the Brontës. After a rainy afternoon playing with toy soldiers, the Brontës began writing the Angria and Glass Town sagas about their toys. In his autobiography, Winston Churchill also notes his preference for childhood play with toy soldiers. A. A. Milne famously penned *Winnie-the-Pooh* (1926) to bring his son's toys to life, and his work in turn has inspired a wave of popular Pooh toys and adaptations. Milne's twentieth-century contemporaries also explored the "lives" of children's toys: Margery Williams's *The Velveteen Rabbit* (1922) is in a direct line that leads to the Toy Story franchise and subsequent Golden Books and picture books; many examples appear in the de Grummond. For a glimpse at American doll culture and manufacture, the de Grummond's Emilie Blackmore Stapp Doll Collection (1936–1960s) incorporates over four hundred dolls that this children's book author, editor, and philanthropist gathered from friends in America and around the world. A close study of dolls reveals attitudes about gender, class, and race. Florence and Bertha Upton's Golliwogg stories (1895–1909) promoted dolls whose exaggerated features would be considered racist today. They reflect the 1890s cultural moment when colonization of Africa was proceeding rapidly.

Beyond linking reading and play, toys also prepare children for their adult roles. Even the apparatus packed with the games offer lessons. To avoid the taint of gambling, for instance, eighteenth-century games often included a teetotum, a spinning top with numbers on its outer edge, instead of dice. By the twentieth century, games like Monopoly (1935) were more interested in teaching capitalism than morality. In its original form as The Landlord's Game from 1903, it was supposed to teach the evils of greed, but Parker Brothers took the game in a new direction.

Games have sometimes inspired fiction for children, such as Eric Weiner's 1990s book series based on the Parker Brothers' game Clue, but more commonly, literary texts inspire toys and games. Card games such as Fairy Tale Families (c. 1987) appropriate and adapt the Grimms' tales, a practice continuing with Wizard of Oz: Yellow Brick Road Game (1999) in which players race to collect ruby slippers, a diploma, a medal of courage, and a heart so that Glinda can grant Dorothy's wish. The sport of Quidditch, invented by J. K. Rowling in her Harry Potter series, has inspired a real-life version with college and university teams around the world.

Toys also reflect their cultural moment. Cold War militarism fueled the growth of the action-figure industry and the popularity of G.I. Joe, Stratego, Axis & Allies, and Battleship. In the early 2000s, a call to encourage children to excel in math and science promoted STEM toys (those designed to foster skills in science, technology, engineering, and math). This led to a new wave of chemistry sets, puzzling toys, and a fresh interest in building implements from Legos to Lincoln Logs. Even Legos connect to literature as seen in *Lego Harry Potter: Building the Magical World* (2011), a book in which players can study the minifigures of the Harry Potter collection and see guides to building structures from the book and film franchise using Lego blocks.

The de Grummond also features anthologies of parlor and outdoor games, helping parents channel children's energy into healthful play. Antonio Blitz's *The Boys' Own Book of Indoor Sports and Choice Parlor games* (189-?) and George Henry Sandison's *How to Behave and How to Amuse: A Handy Manual of Etiquette and Parlor Games in Two Parts* (c. 1895) reveal how games teach teamwork, perseverance, and good sportsmanship. These types of games relate to the school-story tradition popularized in works

A Go-Hawk doll from the Emilie Blackmore Stapp Collection, based on Stapp's *The Trail of the Go-Hawks* (1908). Photograph by Kelly Dunn.

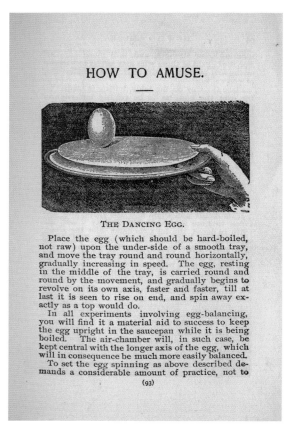

HOW TO AMUSE.

—

THE DANCING EGG.

Place the egg (which should be hard-boiled, not raw) upon the under-side of a smooth tray, and move the tray round and round horizontally, gradually increasing in speed. The egg, resting in the middle of the tray, is carried round and round by the movement, and gradually begins to revolve on its own axis, faster and faster, till at last it is seen to rise on end, and spin away exactly as a top would do.

In all experiments involving egg-balancing, you will find it a material aid to success to keep the egg upright in the saucepan while it is being boiled. The air-chamber will, in such case, be kept central with the longer axis of the egg, which will in consequence be much more easily balanced.

To set the egg spinning as above described demands a considerable amount of practice, not to

(93)

Page from *How to Behave and How to Amuse* (1895) by G. H. Sandison. Courtesy of the de Grummond Collection.

such as Thomas Hughes's *Tom Brown's Schooldays* (1857), L. T. Meade's *A World of Girls* (1886), and the Harry Potter series (1997–2007), in which sports and games figure prominently.

The way books themselves become toys offers a threshold for considering literacy acquisition and learning through play. Nineteenth-century books aimed at the Christmas market were often characterized as "toy books" (e.g., Walter Crane's *The Frog Prince* [1874] is part of the Routledge's Shilling Toy Book series). The twentieth century's increasingly popular pop-up books blurred the line between books and toys further, from *Little Red Ridinghood* (c. 1934) to works by Robert Sabuda. Books utilize interactive elements such as flaps (Molly Idle's *Flora and the Flamingo* [2013] or H. A. Rey's *Anybody at Home* [c. 1939]), and books with sensory appeal are even more like playthings (Dorothy Kunhardt's *Pat the Bunny* [1940]; and *Tony Sarg's Surprise Book: Look, Listen, Smell, Taste and Feel: Open This Book—It Will Open Your Eyes—for Each of Your Senses It Brings a Surprise!* [c. 1941]). Inviting child players to experience the broader world and examine its parts in miniature, toy books can appeal to readers seeking physical engagement with a text, such as Ray Marshall and John Bradley's *The Car: Watch It Work by Operating the Moving Diagrams!* (1984). Roger Nannini's *Josephine's Toy Shop* (1991), for instance, can be unfolded and reassembled as a toyshop, extending the narrative landscape through play.

As the de Grummond Collection bears out, there are many examples of the ways in which games and literature are mutually constitutive and informing. These artifacts reflect their cultural moment and the values adult producers and purchasers want children to consume. The long relationship between books and toys, books as toys, and toys inspired by books demonstrates the rich afterlives of literary texts, the scripts they suggest, and the ways child consumers could appropriate and manipulate characters and themes from their reading.

Chapter 10

Picture Book Art

Nathalie op de Beeck

Picture books are invested in the illusion of simplicity and in active reading practice. Their creators paint surroundings in broad strokes to convey essential details and impel a narrative forward. Readers take in visual details and written captions as they pause on each page, then move on. When we dive into a dramatic maritime adventure by Edward Ardizzone, a slapstick romp by Hans Augusto and Margret Rey, an onomatopoeic soundscape of a here-and-now midcentury city by Margaret Wise Brown, or a snowy Scandinavian-inspired outing with Jan Brett, we participate in what picture book historians have called "the drama of the turning of the page" (Bader 1).

Balancing concise sentences and eye-catching images, the true picture book is a development of late-nineteenth and early-twentieth-century print culture. Ideally, a picture book may be recognized by its visual and verbal interplay across a multipage sequence. Maurice Sendak, in reference to the influential work of Randolph Caldecott, formulated a concise definition of the medium: "Words are left out—but the picture says it. Pictures are left out—but the words say it" (21). In some cases, words other than those in a title are left out altogether: H. A. Rey's comic wordless sequence *Zebrology* (1937) details how zebras came to be, from an initial pairing of a black and a white horse to horse couples who first are bisected white and black, then black and white in strict quadrants, and ultimately striped. (This mock-evolutionary jest, created in the 1930s, surely exists

Illustration from H. A. Rey's *Zebrology* (1937). Courtesy of the de Grummond Collection.

in an awareness of racial implications, even if H. A. Rey did not intend such a possible reading.)

Picture book precursors include the illuminated manuscript and the hornbook, the chapbook and the primer, the illustrated newspaper and the abecedary. Early picture books were hand-colored in an assembly-line manner, supplemented with shiny tipped-in color pages, or presented on pages that alternated between black-and-white and four-color printing. As paper coatings, inks, and lithographic technologies improved and mass printing became cheaper, the picture book took on new possibilities as an affordable (and disposable) nursery item, and greeting cards and colorful broadsides proliferated; artists like Kate Greenaway saw their popular imagery pirated by individuals and companies for use as decoration in the domestic space . Pop-up elements, die-cuts and shaped pages, and "indestructible" cloth or board construction likewise blurred the lines

The letter "E" from Mary Frances Ames's *An ABC for Baby Patriots* (1899). Courtesy of the de Grummond Collection.

between reading and manipulating books. The British company Frederick Warne and Co. and the American company McLoughlin Bros. hybridized toys and texts in myriad puzzles, games, and maps that meant to marry education and play.

As a mode of communication and a source of information, picture books tend to be associated with delivering functional literacy in appealing packages, the more colorful the better. They take a child reader "from instruction to delight," with an emphasis on that unrestrained delight, ease, and novelty. Common assumptions hold that an unambiguous picture may substitute for a basic printed word to help children learn to read, and that picture books thus serve young people in a salutary manner. Yet image/text relationships and representational conventions are complex. Political designs are never far from picture books, however innocent the style in which they are written and drawn, and as children read, they are informed that specific words and pictures belong together and make sense as symbolic units. Scholars including Perry Nodelman and Patricia Crain have explored what it means for preliterate humans to figure out that, say, "A Is for Apple" and that two-dimensional shapes on a page can represent letters, words, three-dimensional objects, and abstract ideas. Critic Joe

Sutliff Sanders reminds us that picture books typically are "chaperoned" texts, provided by an adult gatekeeper to a young person.

Because we read them with decades of hindsight (and occasional dismay), archival picture books like those held in the de Grummond Collection sometimes undermine residual faith in a one-to-one correspondence between symbol and representation and in picture books as wholesome fare. For instance, in Mary Frances Ames's 1898 British picture book, *An ABC for Baby Patriots*, contemporary readers discover the overt ideological and in this case imperial subtexts of a pictorial ABC. One spread—for the letter E—pictures a child in a helmet and a jet-black poodle sitting on its haunches, regarding a globe mapping the continents. Ames composes a stanza—"E is our Empire / Where sun never sets; / The larger we make it / The bigger it gets"—referencing a cliché about the British Empire's relentless growth, while visually implying a power dynamic between the child and dog. In Ames's letter-G spread, a man aims a rifle at a flock of geese to illustrate "G is the Game / We preserve with such care / To shoot, as it gracefully / Flies through the air." Here, elegant birds are cultivated in order to be killed for sport by privileged and well-armed hunters. Each example asserts Victorian nationalism and entitlement and shows how an ABC book—which includes print and script letters for children to trace and learn—is a tool not only for literacy but for culture. Archival picture books reveal commonplaces of eras, and childhoods, that are no longer our own.

In the mid-twentieth century, library professionals signaled the professionalization of the contemporary picture book by awarding prizes to picture book art, with the Caldecott Medal in the United States first going to Dorothy P. Lathrop for *Animals of the Bible* in 1938 and the Greenaway Medal in England first going to Edward Ardizzone's *Tim All Alone* in 1957. With an extensive collection of original manuscripts and art, the de Grummond's archive includes materials from well-known picture book authors and illustrators, including Caldecott winners such as Barbara Cooney, Berta and Elmer Hader, Marcia Brown, Robert McCloskey, Margaret Wise Brown, and Emily Arnold McCully; Coretta Scott King Illustrator Award winners such as E. B. Lewis; and many others. Author-illustrator Esphyr Slobodkina, best known for her popular 1940 picture book *Caps for Sale*, donated a significant collection of materials to the de Grummond and completed a large wall mural for the University of Southern Mississippi in 1970.

Picture books thus benefit critical study and reveal much about how childhood was experienced by past generations. In the retold stories of tippler Rip Van Winkle, endangered Red Riding Hood, or tragic Cock Robin, we now notice the ways familiar characters go through predictable motions. In the subtle civil rights–era work of Ezra Jack Keats, famous for *The Snowy Day* and an African American protagonist named Peter, we see homespun portraits of childhood, and we likely consider the lack of diverse racial representation in literature for all children. In the naturalistic studies of Robert McClung or Jim Arnosky, we find an appreciation for the insects, birds, and other wildlife whose life stories are taken for granted in times of new technologies. Picture books help us recognize how notions considered appropriate for past generations of children can shift. They suggest the attitudes and surroundings that are commonplace among children and their gatekeepers today. They also stand in close proximity to their cousins like the comic strip, the graphic narrative, and the digital text. Even as they are perceived as educational entertainment, picture books provide a wealth of childhood history, a medium for sequential art and design, and a delivery system for societal norms.

Chapter 11

CHILDREN'S NONFICTION

Jennifer Brannock and Andrew Haley

A recent article recommending informational books for children was titled "12 Nonfiction Books Kids Will Actually Read," and the implied slight is nothing new: children's nonfiction is rarely given as much love as children's fiction (Riedel). School libraries collect biographies of Harriet Tubman, but no one expects historical biography will outsell Harry Potter, and books on meteorology will never be cherished like *The Snowy Day* (1962). Not surprisingly, only six "informational" children's books have won a Newbery Award (although the first winner in 1922 was historical nonfiction). In 1976 Milton Meltzer concluded that prize committees view nonfiction works as if they had no more literary value than the "Sears Roebuck catalog or the telephone directory," and while new prizes recognize nonfiction children's literature, Meltzer's description is still more true than not (n.p.). However, children's nonfiction has introduced generations to acrobats, baseball, and chemistry; taught face painting, geography, and husbandry; explained rockets, sex, and *T. rexes*; and sparked interest in x-rays, yodeling, and zoos. These books taught us to build model planes and to ski, told us how many miles separated the earth and its moon, counted the teeth in a great white shark, and cut away the walls of a castle to expose the dungeon at its core. Grounded in reality, they nonetheless inspire. Now, collections such as the de Grummond Children's Literature Collection serve scholars by documenting what adults think children should know and by demonstrating the creativity

Turkish Delight.

Here is a sweet that sounds really difficult. But it only wants a little care in following directions exactly. It is rather more trouble to make than some sweets, but it is well worth it. And just think of producing a box of lovely sugared-all-over Delight, and saying you made it yourself!

You will see, when you look at the receipe below, that the gelatine has to soak for two hours. So you might put it to soak, if you like, before you go out, or while you are doing something else, because you don't want to stand waiting for two hours while the gelatine is getting soft. You might even put it to soak before you go to bed the night before you want to make your Turkish Delight. It would not matter if it stood longer than two hours, but it must not be a shorter time.

You will need to have ready :—

Two or three Basins.
A Knife.
A Saucepan.
A small Strainer.
A Lemon Squeezer.
A Tablespoon.
½-lb. Icing Sugar.
Cochineal.
1 teaspoonful Citric Acid.
A Teaspoon.
A Teacup.
Two Dinner Plates.
Two Soup Plates.
An Orange.
A Lemon.
1 lb. Granulated Sugar.
1 ounce Leaf Gelatine.
One teacupful Cold Water.

29   Adding the Gelatine.

A recipe for Turkish Delight from *The Little Girl's Sweet Book* (1923). Courtesy of the de Grummond Collection.

that children's book authors have invested in telling stories of all things real, both mundane and wondrous.

For instance, expectations that parents have for their daughters (and occasionally their sons) are reflected in children's cookbooks. At the start of the twentieth century, it was assumed that every young girl would eagerly embrace cookery. *When Mother Lets Us Cook* (1909) provides ten-to-twelve-year-old girls instructions so they can teach themselves how to prepare family meals "without troubling mother and the cook too much" (Johnson ix). "Take some cold fish, say enough to make 1 pint, and pick it to pieces with a silver fork," the cookbook advises girls, who are instructed in making scalloped fish by whipping up a cream sauce from a roux and baking the concoction in a "pretty hot oven" for about fifteen minutes. Flora Klickmann's *The Little Girl's Sweet Book* shows a young girl, unsupervised, cooking over a hot stov

A generation later in the era of the can opener, young girls, Sherri Inness argues, required more convincing to spend a hot afternoon in the kitchen (Inness 127). Postwar cookbooks like *The Seventeen Cookbook* (1964) claimed cooking was fun, provided tastier recipes, and promised more tangible rewards. "Few things enhance a girl's stock as a girl as swiftly, as surely, as something really good to eat that she has made herself," *The Seventeen Cookbook* assured readers (Inness 128). And another postwar cookbook, *Date Bait* (1952), was even more direct: "Does Suzy have all the boys hanging around her place like a school of fish around a worm, just because of a certain cake she bakes? Nothing to it—you can hook those fish in a jiffy" (Inness 127–28).

Cookbooks were generally—although not always—written for young women, and books on space travel were often—although not always—addressed to boys. Carla Greene's *I Want to Be a Space Pilot* (1961) introduces children to the science of space travel through a fictional frame story in which a young boy named Kip discusses becoming an astronaut with his father, an atmosphere-bound pilot. *I Want to Be a Space Pilot* and other Cold War books on space travel, such as William P. Gottlieb's *Space Flight and How it Works* (1963), generally presented factual information about planets, orbits, rocketry, and gravity to young minds eager to contribute to flag and country, and accuracy and supporting evidence remain an important quality in nonfiction literature. As Diane L. Barlow wrote in the 1990s, "it is critical that children's books present biological information accurately" if you want children to "consider biology as a career" (Barlow 166). But even the soberest accounts occasionally included a flight of fancy. In *The First Book of Space Travel* (1953), Jeanne Bendick cautiously speculated that there may be life on other planets: "Are there intelligent beings on other planets in our solar system? Most scientists say no, but we can't be sure. . . . It is fun to imagine our kind of humans on other worlds, but they would probably look so different that we might not recognize them

The wet concrete poured out of the bucket of the mixer. All day long it filled and dumped, filled and dumped, making a new, white road of wet concrete. Behind the mixer came the finishing machine with its long smooth blade. It moved forward slowly, smoothing and patting the wet concrete to make it strong and hard. Last of all came the men with the long handled brooms. They swept back and forth, like great fingers, so the road wouldn't be too smooth and the cars wouldn't skid in the rain.

as people at all" (58). The book's illustrator was less reserved. The text is accompanied by a drawing of astronauts greeting a humanoid red Martian with an ingratiating smile—a liberty that surely sparked the imagination of readers and spurred greater interest in science. And that was the goal. During the Cold War, the US government, anticommunist zealots, and, as Julia Mickenberg argues, even leftist opponents of the Cold War (who believed that teaching the scientific method could end war and racism) promoted science education (Mickenberg 204–20).

Page from *Benny the Bulldozer* by Edith Thacher Hurd, illustrated by Clement Hurd (1947). Courtesy of the de Grummond Collection.

Few subjects have failed to find a children's book publisher, including topics once considered taboo. "In recent years," James Cross Giblin observed in 2000, "nonfiction writers have explored in a frank, thoroughgoing manner such subjects as child abuse, teenage sex and pregnancy, abortion, homosexuality, and substance abuse—despite lingering opposition from groups of various stripes who believe that such books are unsuitable for children and young adults" (n.p.).

The de Grummond Collection documents the appearance of these books on once-forbidden topics, but it also provides fertile ground for scholars exploring subtler leitmotifs that may offer insight into the zeitgeist. Francesca Russello Ammon's groundbreaking work on *Benny the Bulldozer* (1947) and other postwar American children's books featuring construction vehicles demonstrate the ways in which historians can excavate the past. Ammon argues that the proliferation of "bulldozer books" helped "a younger generation to make sense of the world around them as their environment underwent massive physical upheaval" during the building of the interstate highway system in the 1950s and urban renewal projects of the 1960s (307). Relying on research and photography provided by the construction industry, children's literature supported the "culture of clearance" by suggesting that bulldozers could tame nature without negative consequences and by turning the manly construction worker (or the anthropomorphized machine) into a heroic figure (315, 319).

The preservation of informational children's books—both popular and more obscure titles—opens other avenues for study. In the adult world, nonfiction banishes the fictional (with some celebrated exceptions), but children's books regularly blur the lines that demark genres (Giblin n.p.). Biographies may make up dialogue (and adjust language to be appropriate for the age of the reader) and educational books like *I Want to Be a Space Pilot* feature fictional narrators. These techniques are controversial and rich subjects for literary scholarship. The Childhood of Famous Americans series, first published in 1932, recounts the childhoods of well-known Americans including Abraham Lincoln, Pocahontas, and Eleanor Roosevelt—and was never averse to putting words in Lincoln's mouth. Lena de Grummond authored several biographies for the series, including books on Babe Didrikson, Jefferson Davis, and Jean Felix Piccard, and the

Collection documents the series' evolution. Early works featured founders, politicians, and men of war—with only a handful of women and people of color—but recent volumes profile diverse lives, including Wilma Rudolph, Amelia Earhart, Martin Luther King Jr., and Mahalia Jackson.

The Collection features manuscripts from children's book authors that include research materials, drafts, illustrations, and correspondence with publishers, editors, and fans. The popular science writer and editor Herbert Zim penned over one hundred books and created and edited the popular Golden Guides science series. For Zim's book *The Universe* (1961), researchers can view all three published editions of the book, drafts with Zim's edits, and research materials, including a copy of "A New Scientific Instrument in the Making" published by the US Naval Research Laboratory about the Sugar Grove Telescope and a four-page list of general astronomy and science books he consulted. And Zim is only one of dozens of authors who have contributed manuscripts to the nonfiction collection. The Margaret O. Hyde Papers include manuscripts of her space and science books, such as *Atoms Today and Tomorrow* (1955), *Exploring Earth and Space: The Story of the I.G.Y.* (1957), and *Medicine in Action, Today and Tomorrow* (1964). And Vicki Cobb, a popular author of applied science books, donated manuscript materials from several of her books. Dubbed "the Julia Child of hands-on science," her titles take science one step further through experiments that can be done at home. The de Grummond Collection makes it possible to consider how an author's research and writing process shapes the way we construct the world for children.

Chapter 12

AFRICAN AMERICAN CHILDREN'S LITERATURE AND WRITERS

Deborah D. Taylor

The history of African American books for young people has been an ongoing struggle to counter negative images and stereotypes about Black people that have been pervasive in the United States throughout the years. As Jonda McNair notes in her July 2018 article in *Horn Book*, "In 1919, when W. E. B. Du Bois announced the arrival of *The Brownies' Book*, one of the first magazines created primarily for Black children, the 'children of the sun,' he outlined seven goals for the publication, two of which were 'to make them [Black children] familiar with the history and achievements of the Negro race' and 'to make them know that other colored children have grown into beautiful, useful, and famous persons'" (n.p.). In the introduction to her book, *Image of the Black in Children's Fiction* (1973), Dorothy Broderick quotes Sterling A. Brown from his book *The Negro in American Fiction* (1937): "Negro children have generally been written of in the same terms as their mothers and fathers, as quaint, living jokes, designed to make white children laugh" (3). Brown lists five books different from that trend: *Araminta* (1935) and *Jerome Anthony* (1936) by Eva Knox Evans; *Popo and Fifina* (1932) (in collaboration with legendary poet and writer Langston Hughes); and *You Can't Pet a Possum* (1934) and *The Sad-Faced Boy* (1937) by Arna Bontemps, all of which are held in the de Grummond.

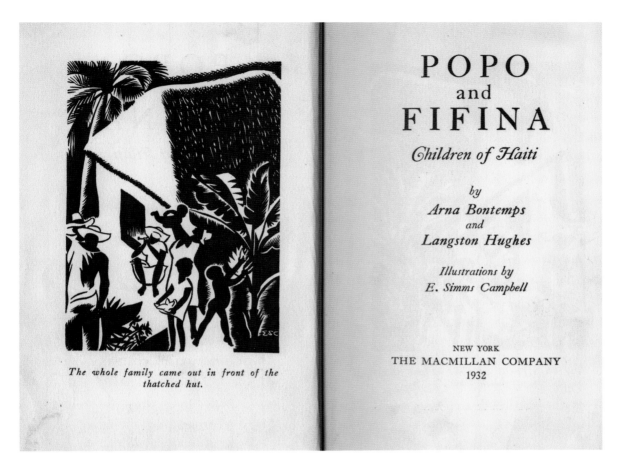

POPO
and
FIFINA

Children of Haiti

by
Arna Bontemps
and
Langston Hughes

Illustrations by
E. Simms Campbell

NEW YORK
THE MACMILLAN COMPANY
1932

The whole family came out in front of the thatched hut.

Bontemps was a renowned African American librarian and writer. Eva Knox Evans was described by Augusta Baker in a 1975 *Horn Book* article as "a white author who was one of the first to portray black children in a normal, everyday atmosphere" (n.p.). Baker was one of many intrepid African American librarians and educators who worked to counter negativity in books that featured Black children. Augusta Baker and her Chicago counterpart Charlemae Hill Rollins recognized there were few positive works they could embrace and comfortably place in the hands of African American children. They also recognized that as white children were exposed to these images, they were developing a false sense of African Americans. Rollins, born in Yazoo City, Mississippi, began her work in

Frontispiece and title page from *Popo and Fifina: Children of Haiti* by Arna Bontemps and Langston Hughes, illustrated by E. Simms Campbell (1932). Courtesy of the de Grummond Collection.

My! gasped Araminta as she pulled herself up.

Page from *Araminta* by Eva Knox Evans, illustrated by Erick Berry (1935). Courtesy of the de Grummond Collection.

1927 at the Harding Square Branch of the Chicago Public Library; Baker joined the New York Public Library in 1937.

Both of these librarians were trailblazers in promoting books about and for African American children. In addition to exposing negative images, they also highlighted materials that were exemplary. Rollins produced one of the first important publications on African American books for children: a first edition of *We Build Together, A Reader's Guide to Negro Life and Literature for Elementary and High School Use*, published in 1941 by the National Council of Teachers of English, is held in de Grummond. This publication served to educate librarians and teachers on how to select books about Black children and included an extensive annotated bibliography. Rollins also wrote and edited the kinds of books she thought would resonate with African American youth, including biographies of famous African Americans and a unique collection in 1963: *Christmas Gif': An Anthology of Christmas Songs, Poems, and Stories Written by and about African Americans*. An updated edition of this work was published in 1993 with illustrations by Ashley Bryan. Augusta Baker contributed to the field by publishing in 1957 *Books about Negro Life for Children*, a bibliography of the extensive book collection she acquired for her branch. In the aforementioned 1975 *Horn Book* article, Baker posed some important questions: "Are books providing positive identification for black children? Are white children seeing a true picture of the ethnic, cultural, and historical aspects of black Americans? Does fiction lack the black perspective which can be acquired from an understanding of and appreciation for the black experience? Does one have to live the black experience in order correctly to portray it?" (n.p.).

Baker's concerns were some of the same issues that propelled two librarians, Glyndon Flynt Greer and Mabel McKissick, to establish the Coretta Scott King Book Awards in 1969 to provide recognition for African American authors and later illustrators of books for children and teen readers. The Coretta Scott King Book Award has a full and rich tradition of recognizing the best literature for young people created by African American writers and illustrators. The honored books are of the highest literary and artistic quality and share the universal themes that celebrate the humanity of all. On the journey of nearly fifty years of history, the

That was Christmas, sure enough.
Snow knee-deep an' coastin' fine,
Frozen mill-ponds all ashine,
Seemin' jest to lay in wait,
Beggin' you to come an' skate.
An' you'd git your gal an' go
Stumpin' cheerily thro' the snow,
Feelin' pleased an' skeert an' warm
'Cause she had a-holt yore arm.
Why, when Christmas come in, we
Spent the whole glad day in glee,
Havin' fun an' feastin' high
An' some courtin' on the sly.
Bustin' in some neighbor's door
An' then suddenly, before
He could give his voice a lift,
Yellin' at him, "Christmas gift."
Now sich things are never heard,
"Merry Christmas" is the word.
But it's only change o' name,
An' means givin' jest the same.
There's too many new-styled ways
Now about the holidays.
I'd jest like once more to see
Christmas like it used to be!

Paul Laurence Dunbar

62

63

awards have also introduced, promoted, and encouraged some of the most remarkable creative talent in the field of children's publishing. Still, there are many stories that need to be told and outstanding books need to be promoted and purchased for schools, libraries, and all places that connect with children. The fact that those concerned with the state of books about African American children find themselves in a struggle that has lasted for such a long time could be seen as discouraging. It could also be viewed as part of a relentless determination to continue the historic efforts of educators, librarians, and writers who worked tirelessly in the cause of Black children's literature.

Illustration accompanying Paul Laurence Dunbar's poem "Speakin' o' Christmas" from Charlemae Robbins's *Christmas Gif'* (1963), with line drawings by Tom O'Sullivan. Courtesy of the de Grummond Collection.

Chapter 13

SOUTHERN CHILDREN'S LITERATURE

Laura Hakala

Since the antebellum era, writers have produced literature specifically about and for southern children. Indeed, some of the United States' most popular books for young people, including Annie Fellows Johnston's *The Little Colonel* (1895) and John Green's *Looking for Alaska* (2005), have southern settings. Typically, critical studies about southern children's literature, such as those by Paula Connolly and Donnarae MacCann, discuss how texts reinforce and/or challenge white supremacist values, but southern children's literature also provides insight into regional constructions of gender, social class, religion, and the environment. In fact, these texts often use childhood to promote agrarian ideals privileging rural, agricultural spaces. As southern children's literature has influenced and been influenced by shifting regional views, many features of the texts have changed over time—and some have not. The de Grummond Collection offers valuable resources to better understand this evolution.

During the antebellum era, children's literature from all regions had didactic intentions, but southern works taught the "virtues" of slavery to white readers. Consequently, these books masked the horrors of slavery and made "slavery seem innocent," as Robin Bernstein has argued (142). The de Grummond Collection shows how this trend spanned many genres: readers and primers such as *The Southern Primer; or Child's First*

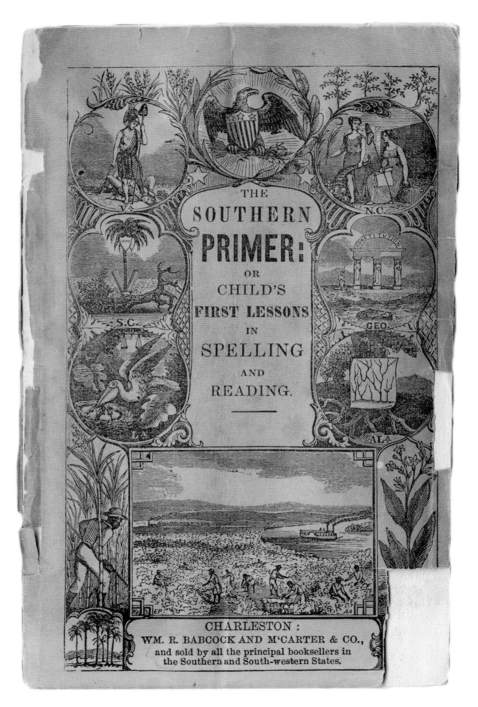

Cover of *The Southern Primer* (1860). Courtesy of the de Grummond Collection.

The front page from the July 1863 issue of *The Children's Friend*.
Courtesy of the de Grummond Collection.

Lessons in Reading and Spelling (1837); domestic novels such as Maria McIntosh's *The Cousins: A Tale of Early Life* (1846) and Louisa Tuthill's *When Are We Happiest?: or, the Little Camerons* (1846); and adventure novels such as Francis Robert Goulding's *Robert and Harold, or, The Young Marooners on the Florida Coast* (1852).

The Civil War intensified efforts to provide white children with a distinct literature promoting southern values. Books and periodicals encouraged children to support secession, help Confederate soldiers, and maintain stability at home. The de Grummond archives contain several periodicals from this era. For example, an 1863 issue of *The Children's Friend*, published by the Presbyterian Committee of Publication in Richmond, Virginia, discusses paper shortages and indicates how Confederate publishing persevered in spite of wartime limitations ("Editorial"). Another periodical published in Macon, Georgia, *Burke's Weekly for Boys and Girls*, reveals how Confederate nationalism continued in the immediate postwar period. In a serialized story, Byrd Lyttle's *Ellen Hunter: A Story of the War* (1868), the narrator declares, "The war is over. The cause, so nobly fought for, lost! But who shall say it is forever" (414). Through reading, southern white children could resurrect the Confederacy in their imaginations.

In the late nineteenth and early twentieth centuries, postbellum plantation fiction accepted the lost cause and romanticized plantation life. Novels by writers such as Thomas Nelson Page and Louise Clarke Pyrnelle idealize a benevolent bond between white children and older enslaved adults who speak in dialect, such as mammies. The de Grummond Collection includes a variation on this trope: a girl mammy. In an obscure six-book series by Joel Chandler Harris, starting with the novel *Little Mr. Thimblefinger* (1894), twelve-year-old Drusilla is "nurse" and "playmate" for two younger white children; however, Drusilla is "more of a child than either Sweetest Susan or Buster John" (5–6). As Drusilla demonstrates, plantation novels use childhood to reinforce racist hierarchies. These books also promote plantations as sites with outdoor spaces large enough for children—both enslaved and slaveholder—to play and have fun. These features appear in the popular Elsie Dinsmore series (1867–1905) by Ohio writer Martha Finley, indicating that we can view literature as "southern" even when authors live outside the region. Ultimately, postbellum plantation fiction constructed a South more imagined than real and socialized generations of white child readers into Jim Crow values.

A major shift happened near the end of the nineteenth century: some children's writers began to depict black southern children in more realistic and empowering ways. For instance, the de Grummond contains some of the first books written for black children, such as Paul Laurence Dunbar's *Little Brown Baby* (1895) and Mary White Ovington's *Hazel* (1913). Hazel particularly breaks stereotypes as a middle-class, educated black girl from Boston sent to live with her grandmother in Alabama. By the time of the civil rights movement, children's books commonly criticized racial

Animals play music. Illustration from 1911 edition of *Nights with Uncle Remus* by Joel Chandler Harris. Courtesy of the de Grummond Collection.

inequality in the South, as Mildred Taylor's series about the Logan family does, and celebrated black childhood, as Jill Krementz's nonfiction picture book *Sweet Pea: A Black Girl Growing Up in the Rural South* (1969) does. Depicting Sweet Pea rolling down hills and climbing trees, Krementz offers a new perspective on agrarianism: black southern children now can choose to enjoy the South's rural landscapes rather than work on them.

As in *Sweet Pea*, contemporary southern books represent diverse childhoods. While most nineteenth-century books focus on the Deep South, twentieth- and twenty-first-century texts explore the South's subregions. Lois Lenski contributed to this trend with novels set in different regions, such as Newbery Medal winner *Strawberry Girl* (1945) about Florida. The de Grummond Collection contains manuscripts and research for many of Lenski's books. Other authors emphasize the South's cultural, racial, and class variations, such as Cynthia Rylant's books set in Appalachia, Kim Siegelson's picture books about the Gullah-Geechee culture of coastal Georgia and South Carolina, and Kathi Appelt's stories about Louisiana bayous. The majority of southern children's books still depict southern childhood as a white or black experience; however, books like Cynthia Kadohata's *Kira-Kira* (2004), about two Japanese-American sisters in Georgia, allow us to consider global influences on the South and its multiethnic communities.

In his introduction to the *Southern Quarterly's* issue on southern childhood, Mark I. West notes another prevalent theme in contemporary southern children's literature: "the tension between the Old South and the New South" (8). In particular, the de Grummond Collection provides insight into the ways child characters resist the Old South by participating in the civil rights movement in Mississippi: the archives contain drafts and manuscripts of Augusta Scattergood's *Glory Be* (2012) and Deborah Wiles's *Freedom Summer* (2001) and *Revolution* (2014). Southern historical experiences appeal to children's and young adult writers, publishers, and readers because they continue to shape conversations about race in America. Ultimately, we can use the de Grummond Collection to identify how the past lingers in contemporary southern books and to examine the roles southern children—both real readers and imagined characters—played in constructing regional values.

Chapter 14

Contemporary Children's and Young Adult Writers

Ramona Caponegro

The term "contemporary" can be nearly as difficult to define as the field of children's literature, but for the purposes of this chapter, the contemporary era commenced in approximately 1960, the beginning of a decade of enormous cultural change in the United States and in publishing. Like other major periods in the history of children's literature, the contemporary era has been marked by tremendous growth and new developments related to the marketplace, technology, storytelling techniques, and understandings of audience, but it has also been uniquely defined by diversification and professionalization.

Since the introduction of New Realism in the 1960s, contemporary writers have been able to explore an increasingly vast array of topics, many of which were previously taboo in works for young readers. Cathryn M. Mercier points out the many challenges in defining realism, particularly in children's literature, noting "parallels" between the difficulties in defining the genre of realism and the field of children's literature (198). Nevertheless, Louise Fitzhugh's *Harriet the Spy* (1964) is often held up as an example of New Realism within children's literature in that this novel features characters confronting social problems—including sexism, classism, bullying, and hypocrisy—and having to define themselves, at least partially, in relation to these social realities. Because of their target audience, young adult novels, such as Robert Cormier's *The Chocolate War* (1974) with its depiction of violence and adult corruption, are able to offer even harsher portrayals of reality and the potentially dire consequences of principled choices and actions than works intended for younger readers, such as *Harriet the Spy*.

Just as contemporary children's literature has come to encompass previously forbidden topics, the field has also expanded to include a greater diversity of characters and children's book creators. Though Ezra Jack Keats was not the first author/illustrator to feature a child of color in a children's book, Keats's *The Snowy Day* (1962) is a milestone in multicultural children's literature, and its original illustrations, along with Keats's papers and material from thirty-seven of his books, reside in the de Grummond Collection. The work of individuals such as Keats and organizations such as the Council on Interracial Books for Children and We Need Diverse Books, as well as the creation and promotion of multicultural book awards, have increased the representation of marginalized people in children's literature. However, the annual publishing statistics on children's books about people of color released by the Cooperative Children's Book Center reveal that more works about and especially by people of color are needed in order to provide young readers with more depictions of varied perspectives and experiences, as well as a fuller understanding of the United States and the people who live here.

The de Grummond Collection not only houses many diverse works of children's literature, but its holdings also include different approaches to multicultural children's literature. For example, the Collection contains two early versions of illustrations from Don Freeman's picture book *Corduroy* (1968), a story that Corinne Duyvis would categorize as a work of "incidental diversity" because it features an African American child selecting a teddy bear without making the child's racial identity central to the story (Duyvis n.p.). The Collection also holds proofs and a typescript for Beverley Naidoo's novel *Journey to Jo-burg: A South African Story* (1985), which can be categorized as an "issues book" for its portrayal of racism and its consequences in South Africa. Just as young readers need to encounter diverse characters and perspectives within books, they also need books that introduce diverse characters and their varied stories in different ways.

While children's literature has slowly become more diverse, the field has professionalized rapidly in the current era. Children's publishing has grown into a larger and more profitable industry, even as major publishing houses have consolidated and self-publishing has skyrocketed over the past few decades. Careers within the field—including agents, editors, reviewers, and book promoters—have expanded, as has the academic study of children's literature. Moreover, the creation of graduate-level writing programs specifically for aspiring children's authors; the Society of Children's Book Writers and Illustrators, the Highlights Foundation, and other organizations devoted to crafting and promoting children's literature; and children's book museums and collections, such as the de Grummond, have also increased the professionalization of children's literature and the careers and expectations of its writers. Some examples of this contemporary professionalization can be seen in the publishers' correspondence, reviews, and promotional materials that are included in many of the authors' and illustrators' papers in the de Grummond Collection. Additionally, some of the children's book creators whose works and papers reside in the de Grummond have worked with the most influential contemporary editors, such as Ursula Nordstrom, Annis Duff, Margaret McElderry, Arthur Levine, David Levithan, and Jason Low.

This increased professionalization has led to the establishment of different literary categories and genres in contemporary times. For example, while Roberta Seelinger Trites argues that Louisa May Alcott's *Little Women* (1868) and Mark Twain's *Adventures of Huckleberry Finn* (1885) "shared in the creation of the adolescent reform novel" (xiii), Michael Cart claims that S. E. Hinton's *The Outsiders* (1967) epitomizes "the nascent genre soon to be called 'young adult literature'" (27). Following the publication of *The Outsiders*, the field of young adult literature burgeoned, and the de Grummond Collection houses original materials from Mary Stolz and Richard Peck, pioneers in young adult literature best known for their highly literary and realistic romance and problem novels respectively. Stolz published the majority of her romances in the decade before Hinton wrote *The Outsiders*, though she continued to write for children and teenagers through the 1980s, and Richard Peck crafted problem novels, works of contemporary realism that address social problems, in the 1970s through

(Left manuscript page)

August Chap I   The Teacher's Funeral
       And the Year After That

If your teacher has to die, August isn't a bad time
of year for it. You know August. The corn's earring.
The clover is in full bloom. The Tomatoes are ripening on the vine. There's a little
less evening now, and that's a warning. You want to
live every day twice over because you'll be back in the
jailhouse of school before the end of the month.

Then our teacher Miss Myrt Arbuckle hauled off and
died. It was like a miracle, though she must have been
forty. You should have seen my kid brother's face. It
looked like Lloyd was hearing the music of the spheres.
Being 1O that summer, he was even more ~~apt~~ *willing* to believe
in miracles than I was. ~~and I was sure willing.~~

You couldn't deny Miss Myrt Arbuckle **was** past her prime.
She was hard of hearing in one ear, no doubt deafened
by her own screaming. And she couldn't whup us like
she wanted to. She was a southpaw for whupping, and
she had arthritis in that elbow, so while she could still
whup, it didn't make much of an impression.

Back in the spring when she called up Lester Kriegbaum
for some infraction, he brought a book to the front of
the room and read it over her knee while she ~~flailed~~ *larruped*
away at his ~~other~~ *fat* end.

So when you get right down to it, if you can't hear
and you can't whup, you're better off dead than teaching.
That's how I ~~saw~~ *looked at* it.

(Left) A manuscript page from *The Teacher's Funeral* (2004),
by Richard Peck. Courtesy of the de Grummond Collection.

(Right) A manuscript page from an early draft of *The Fault in
Our Stars* (2012) by John Green. Courtesy of the de Grummond Collection.

(Right manuscript page)

Chapter 1

My mother thought I was depressed.

Whenever you read a cancer booklet or web site or whatever, they
always list *depression* among the side effects of cancer, but in fact
depression is not a side effect of cancer. Depression is a side effect of
dying. (Cancer is also a side effect of dying. Almost everything is, really.)

So my mom took me in to see my Regular Doctor Jim, who agreed
that I was suffering from a clinical depression, and that I mustn't fear the
world, and that therefore my meds should be adjusted and also I should
attend a Support Group twice a week.

This support group featured a rotating cast of characters in various
states of tumor-driven unwellness. Why did the cast rotate? A side effect of
dying.

The support group, of course, was depressing as hell. It met every
Wednesday and Sunday in the basement of a stone-walled Episcopal
Church shaped like a cross. We all sat in a circle right in the middle of the
cross, where the two boards would have met, where the heart of Jesus
would have been.

I noticed this because Patrick, the Support Group Leader and only
person over 18 in the room, talked about the heart of Jesus every freaking
meeting, all about how we were sitting right in his very sacred heart, and
that we should always remember that children with cancer are in God's
heart.

So here's how it always went in God's heart: Everybody walked/
wheeled in, grazed at a decrepit selection of cookies and lemonade, sat *when he*
down in the Circle of Trust, and listened to Patrick recount for the *was how*
thousandth time his depressingly miserable life story: how he had cancer in *old?*
his balls and they thought he was going to die but he didn't die and now
here he is, a full-grown adult in a church basement in the 437th nicest city
in America, divorced, addicted to video games, mostly friendless, eking out
a meager living by exploiting his cancertastic past, slowly working his way
toward a master's degree that will not actually improve his career
prospects, waiting as we all do for the sword of Damocles to give him the
relief that he escaped lo those many years ago when cancer took both of
his nuts but spared what only the most generous soul would call his life.

AND YOU TOO MIGHT BE SO LUCKY! — My introducer was always *A*
Then we introduced ourselves. Name. Age. Diagnosis. And how we're *variation*
doing today. I'm Esther, I say when they get to me. 16. Thyroid. meTASTIC. *on this*
And I'm doing a-okay. *theme.*

the new millennium. Stolz and Peck both wrote within extremely popular genres of young adult literature, but their writing and story-crafting distinguished their works from many similar or imitative books.

In addition to holding the papers of these early luminaries within young adult literature, the de Grummond Collection also contains the papers of Angela Johnson and John Green, more recent giants within this subfield. Like Stolz and Peck, Johnson has written for younger audiences, as well as for adolescents, and her work spans multiple genres, including contemporary realistic fiction, historical fiction, and poetry. Thus far, Green has not written for an audience younger than adolescents, but of the young adult authors discussed here, his name is probably the most familiar to people outside of children's literature. Like Stolz, Peck, and Johnson, his works of contemporary realism have achieved popular and critical acclaim and have won multiple awards. Green was also one of the first young adult authors to connect heavily with his target audience through social media. He and his brother Hank Green created and host a popular video blog channel on YouTube called the VlogBrothers and helped launch an online community, Nerdfighteria, which exists "anywhere where awesome is being done, and worldsuck is reduced" (Nerdfighteria). The de Grummond Collection contains typescripts, notes, and materials related to the creation of Johnson's and Green's published works; Johnson's correspondence, fan mail, and appearance and event materials; and Green's high school and college writing projects.

Like young adult literature, early readers have emerged as a distinct category within children's literature. In 1957 *The Cat in the Hat*, written and illustrated by Dr. Seuss, and *Little Bear*, written by Else Holmelund Minarik and illustrated by Maurice Sendak, respectively launched the Beginner Book series and the I Can Read! series, immeasurably shaping subsequent early readers. The de Grummond Collection contains thousands of cartoons and other works by Syd Hoff, the author of *Danny and the Dinosaur* (1958) and other popular I Can Read! titles. Just as Hoff's drawing style is easily recognizable, works within the young adult and early reader categories often contain identifiable characteristics.

However, these categories have also expanded to include new forms, such as graphic novels, and the divides related to audience expectations (e.g., books for tweens versus teens) and categories (e.g., picture books versus early readers) have become less discernable over time. Even as the boundaries among categories and genres blur and shift as expectations change, the popularity of different genres waxes and wanes. As previously mentioned, works of contemporary realism for young readers became very popular in the 1960s and 1970s, and problem novels, school stories, and stories that focus on everyday issues and concerns remain staples in contemporary children's chapter books. Then, as Sarah L. Schwebel notes, when the sales of children's books dominated the American publishing industry in the mid-1980s and 1990s, "[h]istorical fiction was an important player in this trend" (2), and the blockbuster success of J. K. Rowling's Harry Potter series at the end of the 1990s and throughout the 2000s breathed new life into the fantasy genre. In the children's chapter book market, works of fantasy, historical fiction, and contemporary realistic fiction are joined by works of nonfiction, mysteries, novels in verse, and science fiction, with popularity, sales figures, and critical attention focused on different individual works and genres at different moments.

Throughout these cycles, the de Grummond continues to curate the work of numerous popular and award-winning contemporary writers. The Collection also highlights the longevity and the new lives that can be given to older, beloved characters through the documents in its H. A. and Margret Rey Papers that relate to the licensing, merchandising, translations, and parodies of Curious George. Similarly, Louise Borden's papers include her careful documentation of the creation of *The Journey That Saved Curious George*, which featured research from the de Grummond Collection and introduced new audiences to the Reys' story. Finally, the de Grummond's holdings showcase the influence of new technology on contemporary writers and their work. For example, the Augusta Scattergood Papers contain flash drives that store material related to two novels, assuring writers and readers that however contemporary and future stories are recorded by their creators, the de Grummond will preserve them for future generations.

Chapter 15

Golden Books

Anita Silvey

In 1940 Georges Duplaix, a French emigré, and editor Lucille Ogle of the Artists and Writers Guild teamed up with new upstart publisher Simon & Schuster to produce a series of high-quality, low-priced books. They relied on Western Printers in Racine, Wisconsin, for production, and twelve Little Golden Books debuted in October 1942. They succeeded beyond the wildest expectations of everyone involved. These twenty-five-cent books, with sturdy covers, lavish full-color illustrations, and engaging stories enticed parents to buy them as they shopped in general stores. In less than a year, Simon & Schuster had orders for 4.7 million copies of assorted titles. After World War II, racks of Little Golden Books appeared in supermarkets across the country, exposing parents and children who might never enter a bookstore to affordable children's books (Marcus, *Minders* 164). Consequently, during the late 1940s, 1950s, and 1960s, millions of American households contained libraries of Golden Books.

Eventually, because of their full-color printing and with lots of room for art, Golden Books hired some of the finest American illustrators of the postwar era. The stable of illustrators was legion, including Garth Williams, Richard Scarry, Gustaf Tenggren, and Alice and Martin Provensen. The first star of Little Golden Books, Gustaf Tenggren, joined the Walt Disney studio as it was developing *Snow White*. By the time he left Disney, the artist had absorbed storytelling lessons but wanted the freedom

A selection of Little Golden Books from the de Grummond Collection. Photograph by Kelly Dunn.

that creating his own books allowed. Other animators followed—such as Alice and Martin Provensen and Mary Blair—but few enjoyed Tenggren's popularity with young readers. The first list of twelve Little Golden Books featured two Tenggren selections—*Bedtime Stories* (1942) and his now-classic *The Poky Little Puppy* (1942) (Marcus, *Golden Legacy* 64). In these books and others like *The Saggy Baggy Elephant* (1947) and *Tawny Scrawny Lion* (1952), Tenggren combined surefire audience appeal with brilliant and engaging watercolors of scenes and characters.

During the years leading up to and after the outbreak of World War II, talented artists fled Europe and came to America. Georges Duplaix sent Russian Feodor Rojankovsky enough money to cover his passage to America in return for an exclusive publishing contract (Marcus, *Golden Legacy* 46). Others like Hungarian Tibor Gergely contributed many popular books, such as *Scruffy the Tugboat* (1946). The exodus of talent from Europe also included H. A. and Margret Rey, whose papers are housed in the de Grummond Collection. Any scholars looking to study the effects of World War II on American books for children will find the de Grummond Collection invaluable.

Certainly, one of the most felicitous connections for the list was established by Lucille Ogle with New York's progressive Bank Street School and Writer's Laboratory. Margaret Wise Brown, the star pupil of Bank Street, began providing manuscripts, starting with *The Golden Egg Book* (1947). Although Brown would publish her classic *Goodnight Moon* (1947) with Harper, her Golden Book texts—*The Color Kittens* (1949), with illustrations by the Provensens, and *The Sailor Dog* (1953), featuring art by Garth Williams—stand as some of her best work. Others from Bank Street like Edith Thacher Hurd and Ruth Krauss also added important titles.

For those studying the economics of publishing, Golden Books point to some of the ethical dilemmas in the industry. Although these books made some authors and illustrators household names, the contracts had drawbacks for the creators. Most of them were given a "work for hire" agreement, with only a one-time payment. Although *The Poky Little Puppy* by Janette Sebring Lowrey would become one of the best-selling picture books of all time in the United States, the author received only a $75 flat fee for the manuscript, a loss of revenue that annoyed Lowrey her entire life. Richard Scarry, with art school and the army behind him, entered into an exclusive contract with Golden, agreeing to provide them with several books a year while he got a monthly paycheck. As Scarry's work evolved, he began to fill every available space on a book's page, making his books a feast for young readers' eyes. But this author-illustrator who became as popular as Dr. Seuss did not receive a penny in royalties on his books until 1956. When he finally demanded them, his editor agreed

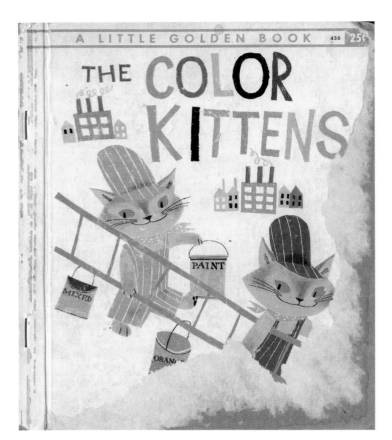

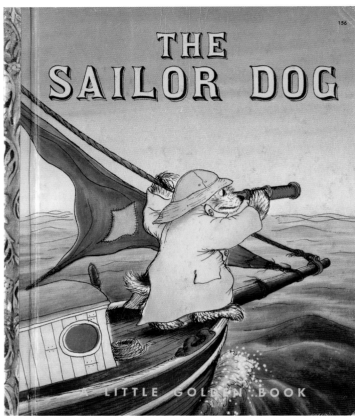

(Left) Cover of *The Color Kittens* by Margaret Wise Brown, illustrated by Martin and Alice Provensen (1949). Courtesy of the de Grummond Collection.

(Right) Cover of *The Sailor Dog* by Margaret Wise Brown, illustrated by Garth Williams (1953). Courtesy of the de Grummond Collection.

to pay him for each book sold, only because he asked (Silvey, *Children's Book-a-Day Almanac* n.p.).

Golden Books often became cherished stories of a lifetime—beloved by average Americans and more famous ones. Caroline Kennedy, daughter of President John F. and Jacqueline Kennedy, adored Ruth Krauss's *I Can Fly* (1951). *New York Times* best-selling author David Macaulay kept his copy of *The Golden Book of Science for Boys and Girls* (1956) into adulthood. Financier Steve Forbes learned to love reading because his mother shared *The Golden Bible for Children: The New Testament* (1951) (Silvey, *Everything* 53, 103). Even Koko the Gorilla, who learned sign language, had a favorite Golden Book, *The Three Little Kittens* (1942) (Patterson, *Koko's Kitten*).

There would be many additions to the Golden Books line over the years—Giant Golden Books, Walt Disney books, television spin-offs (Roy Rogers, Gene Autry, Howdy Doody, Captain Kangaroo), and even books about the Disney Mouseketeers: *Annette: Sierra Summer* (1960). When the space race heated up in the late fifties, Golden Books responded with titles such as *The World of Science* (1958), *Exploring Space* (1958), and *The Giant Golden Book of Mathematics* (1958). Titles about Sesame Street characters included one of the most enduring Golden Books, *The Monster at the End of this Book* (1971), starring Grover. Barbie, Tickle Me Elmo, the Teenage Mutant Ninja Turtles, and Disney movies inspired later books.

But as adored as they were by the masses, Golden Books in all their permutations rarely received the approval of librarians or teachers. In fact, they faced severe librarian resistance. Even with millions in print, the books were often not catalogued or circulated in libraries. In the massive collection of over 1,500 Golden Book items in the de Grummond Collection can be found everything from the original titles to those published over the next eighty years. A combination of popular culture and American commerce, Golden Books have always represented mainstream American society; all of the important social issues of the twentieth century can be researched in their pages—including diversity in children's books or the visible roles of women. Because the de Grummond Collection has preserved so many titles, it contains a treasure trove for researchers who want to explore the most popular American brand ever created for children.

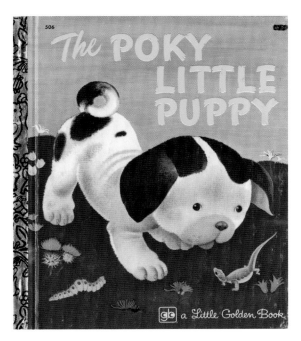

Cover of *The Poky Little Puppy* by Janette Sebring Lowrey, illustrated by Gustaf Tenggren (1942). Courtesy of the de Grummond Collection.

Chapter 16

The H. A. and Margret Rey
Collection

Ann Mulloy Ashmore

Hans Augusto and Margret Rey never set out to write books for children. According to them, success was a happy accident. The opportunity came about when Jacques Schiffrin, an editor at Éditions Gallimard, saw one of Hans's humorous cartoons in a newspaper and asked him if he could create a children's book based on one of the characters. The publication of *Rafi et les 9 singes* [*Rafi and the 9 Monkeys*] (1939), a story about a lonely giraffe befriended by a family of monkeys, led to a second manuscript featuring the antics of one small monkey named Fifi. Today children and parents around the world know him as Curious George.

Both German Jews, originally from Hamburg, Hans first met Margret when he attended a party hosted by her older sister, Mary. After serving in the German army during World War I, Hans was unable to complete his studies at the University of Munich due to the dire economic conditions in Weimar Germany at the time. Urged by his family, Hans left Germany in 1925 to take a position in an import-export firm owned by his brother-in-law, James Mangus, in Rio de Janeiro. Ten years later, Hans met Margret again when she traveled to Rio de Janeiro as a courier bringing cash receipts owed to the Mangus firm. Within three months of Margret's arrival in Brazil the two were married. Hans quit his job at the import-export firm and together they formed their own advertising company. When Margret's parents offered to give the couple a honeymoon in Europe, the two set sail in January 1936, first for London, then Germany to visit both their families and friends. Paris had to wait a year, but once they arrived in February 1937, they made it their home and would have stayed there forever had it not been for the German invasion of France in June 1940.

Following their escape from Paris hours ahead of the German army, the Reys arrived in New York in October 1940. Houghton Mifflin's Grace Hogarth immediately sought a contract for the sequel to *Rafi*. Soon, opportunities came from other publishing houses, including an offer from Ursula Nordstrom, the legendary Director of Harper Books for Boys and Girls. Nordstrom hired Rey to illustrate four books, two of them, *The Polite Penguin* (1941) and *Don't Frighten the Lion* (1942), written by Margaret Wise Brown.

Correspondence between the Reys, their editors, and literary friends span more than four decades and provide a window for researchers into post–World War II children's publishing. Their letters discuss issues such as stereotyping, inclusion, diversity—subjects they discussed at length with Jesse Jackson, author of *Call Me Charley* (Harper and Brothers, 1945), and led to Margret's book *Spotty* (Harper and Brothers, 1945). Likewise, Margret's correspondence with Ursula Nordstrom often commented on opportunities (and the lack thereof) for women in publishing both as authors and as editors—topics that dominated the field in the second half of the twentieth century.

Racial stereotyping became an issue for the Reys with the decision to republish their book *Elizabite* (Harper and Brothers, 1942) in the early 1960s. A humorous tale about an out-of-control carnivorous plant, *Elizabite* included stereotypical depictions of an African American servant in the first edition. These illustrations were removed in the revised edition, according to Hans, in order "to avoid the opprobrium of racism."

The first edition of *Elizabite* is another data point in the history of children's literature, but for a different reason. The manuscript delivered to Nordstrom in June 1941 credited "the verses" to Margret. Nordstrom, however, published the book with only Hans's name on the cover. In an interview forty years later, Margret reflected, "Many books later, perhaps

Illustration from "How the Tortoise Beat the King-Vulture," illustrated by H. A. Rey. Courtesy of the de Grummond Collection.

because of the women's movement, I said, 'Why the hell did I do this? After that, both husband and wife were listed as the authors of the *Curious George* books'" (McKenzie n.p.).

All of these texts are included in the H. A. and Margret Rey Collection at the de Grummond. The scope of Hans and Margret Rey's vast literary estate extends far beyond the field of children's literature, however. Hans's artistic works include not only his early illustrations and publications in Germany and Brazil, but also his commercial advertising art and graphic design work created for the couple's advertising company. Still unpublished and relatively unknown is a set of exquisitely illustrated Brazilian folktales that Hans translated from the native Tupi language into Portuguese.

Later in life, Hans renewed his interests in science, teaching himself celestial cartography. This interest led to the publication of two books for amateur astronomers: *The Stars: A New Way to See Them* (Houghton Mifflin, 1952) and *Find the Constellations* (Houghton Mifflin, 1954). Like the Curious George books, *The Stars* has never been out of print. Environmental issues dominated Hans's last years. During the fuel shortages of 1973, Hans became a staunch advocate for the use of wind power and the adoption of a clean energy policy for the United States. He even used his annual New Year's card in 1974 to send a message for conservation by drawing the couple riding a bicycle past a closed gasoline station.

Already a professional woman prior to her 1935 marriage, Margret managed the business side of the couple's literary career. Her advertising and marketing acumen came from the Berlin office of London's Crawford Advertising Agency. Under the tutelage of Hans Schleger and Arpad Elfer, two of the most influential creative directors in twentieth-century advertising, Margret honed her eye for what constitutes good commercial art, a skill she applied (vociferously, to the dismay of many a printer) during the couple's publishing career. Collections of Margret's photography, needlework, and pottery are also included in their estate. After Hans's death in 1977, Margret devoted her life to maintaining his legacy and the books they created together. The Rey Collection includes numerous examples of her Curious George merchandizing promotions including early filmstrips, "Read-A-Loud" books with vinyl recordings, and many, many variations of stuffed Georges in little red shirts.

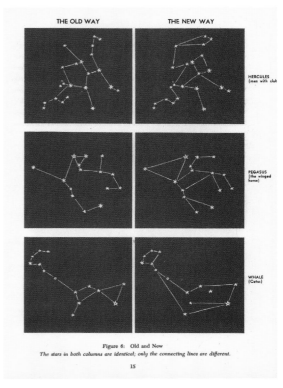

A page from H. A. Rey's *The Stars: A New Way to See Them* (1952). Courtesy of the de Grummond Collection.

all the best from the Reys

14 Hilliard St., Cambridge, Mass.

12-15-73

Here's to Lena !
(Say, can you use proof sheets, for
some of our books ? They are big,
though — whole sheets, in full color).
Thanks for the offer of warm hospitality — maybe
we'll need it.
We were in Europe when
you were up north.
Love,
Margret + Hans

A hand-illustrated 1974 New Year's card from H. A. and Margret Rey to Lena de Grummond. Courtesy of the de Grummond Collection.

One curious note: contrary to the iconic illustration of George carrying books and illustrations to Hattiesburg that decorated Hans's first letter to Lena de Grummond, Margret's will directed the Reys' literary estate to the de Grummond Collection at the University of Mississippi in Oxford by mistake, instead of the University of Southern Mississippi. Happily, as things turned out, it was just another little scrape that George found himself in the middle of and, in the end, turned out well for everyone.

THE EZRA JACK KEATS
COLLECTION

Rudine Sims Bishop

It was not until a quarter of a century after the awarding of the first Caldecott Medal that Ezra Jack Keats's *The Snowy Day* (1962), a story about a young child playing in the snow, became the first picture book featuring a Black child to win the award in 1963. The book was cited not only for its main character but also for Keats's innovative use of varying art techniques and media, especially collage.

Peter, the main character in *The Snowy Day*, was inspired by a series of four photographs of a three- or four-year-old African American boy whom Keats had run across in a *Life* magazine article from the 1940s. In his Caldecott acceptance speech, Keats noted that he was "totally captivated" by the child's "expressive face, his body attitudes, the very way he wore his clothes." He kept the photos, hanging them up in his studio from time to time, thinking that the child could one day be a character in one of his books. That child became Peter, and *The Snowy Day* became a classic.

Although *The Snowy Day* is his best-known work, it was just one of the twenty-two books Keats wrote. He illustrated eighty-five children's books altogether and became one of the best-known and most beloved American illustrators of children's picture books. His major contributions to the field included his innovative art techniques, his trailblazing

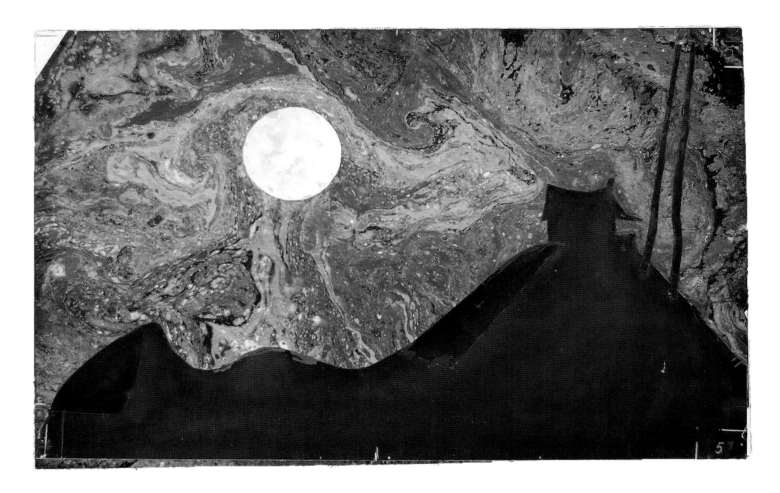

A sample of marbleized paper created by Ezra Jack Keats for *John Henry: An American Legend* (1965), written and illustrated by Keats. Courtesy of the de Grummond Collection.

depiction of a multicultural cast of characters, and his illumination of an urban landscape.

Before *The Snowy Day*, Caldecott Medal winners tended to be painterly; the artists used various paints in their original art—watercolors, oils, tempera, etc. Keats used these media, too, but in telling Peter's story, he followed his own unique artistic impulses. He worked with cut papers of various textures and hues—including marbleized papers that he himself created—to represent figures, clothes, and backgrounds, such as wallpaper, snow-covered hills, and city buildings. His papers came from various places in the world, such as Italy, Sweden, Belgium, and Japan. He

used patterned paper, oilcloth, gum erasers (to stamp snowflakes), India ink, and paints. The effect of using this technique in a book that was so well received was to inspire other illustrators to follow in his footsteps. Decades later, collage is not at all uncommon as a medium to illustrate picture books.

At a time when the world of children's books was, in the words of Nancy Larrick, "all-white," Peter was a novelty—an appealing young Black child enjoying the snow, an experience shared by many children across ethnic and cultural groups. Peter is featured in seven books altogether. In later books he is joined by his little sister Susie, his dog Willie, and friends Amy, Archie (with his cat), Louie, and Roberto. Keats's cast of characters, which includes both boys and girls, is multiethnic: African American, Latinx, Asian American and Caucasian. More importantly, his characters faced problems that are familiar to most children, such as the arrival of a new sibling (*Peter's Chair*); dealing with bullies (*Goggles*);

Original artwork for *Whistle for Willie* (1964), written and illustrated by Ezra Jack Keats. Courtesy of the de Grummond Collection.

Photograph of Ezra Jack Keats drawing for schoolchildren in 1979. Courtesy of the de Grummond Collection.

being brave in the face of potential ridicule (*A Letter to Amy*); helping a friend in need (*Pet Show!*). And their solutions are clever, but not out of reach for ordinary children.

Keats's neighborhood is decidedly urban, which was an unusual setting for the time. Possibly based on Keats's own Brooklyn neighborhood, it is a space of buildings, stoops, empty lots, fences, and graffiti. It is not, however, gloomy; Keats uses color to make the spaces appear warm, even inviting. To Peter and his buddies, it is simply home, the place where they live and play. Very few of the books that won the Caldecott Medal before *The Snowy Day* had an urban setting (*Madeline's Rescue*, set in Paris, is one exception). Keats's use of an urban landscape allowed countless city children to see their lives reflected in literature.

Keats died of a heart attack in 1983, but the Ezra Jack Keats Foundation is dedicated to preserving his work and extending his legacy. The Foundation sponsors programs and awards that build on Keats's work and values, especially his commitment to diversity in children's books. The Foundation offers grants and bookmaking competitions and gives awards to emerging picture book creators. It also sponsors performances and university scholarships. The Foundation partners with the de Grummond Collection at the University of Southern Mississippi, which serves as the sole repository of the Ezra Jack Keats Archive of original manuscripts and illustrations, sketches and dummies, and his papers, including personal and professional correspondence, fan mail, and photographs and memorabilia. As the de Grummond's finding aid notes, "The EJK Awards for new writers and artists are presented at the de Grummond Collection."

Chapter 18

Other Notable de Grummond Collections

Tana Hoban Papers

Tana Hoban first contributed materials to the de Grummond Collection in 1982, and her daughter, Miela Hoban Ford, made a substantial addition to the Collection in 2007, after her mother's death in 2006. In this collection, one gets a feel for Hoban as a person through the diaries she kept; as a commercial photographer through the photos and layouts of advertisements; and as a children's book author through the book dummies for many of her published and unpublished books. For the reader who knows Hoban only as a children's book author, the exploration of her work prior to the publication of her first children's book is an awe-inspiring experience.

Hoban was selected as the only female photographer in *Time* magazine's feature article "Half a Century of U.S. Photography" in 1953. Hoban truly excelled in this art form, more often than not allowing the photographs to speak for themselves rather than depending on text. Her work was designed to encourage children to look at the world around them. Inspired by a short description of an experiment conducted at the Bank Street School in New York City, wherein children were given cameras and asked to photograph what they saw on the way to school, Hoban described her intent in using manufactured and naturally occurring objects in her books, saying, "My books are points of departure to encourage and provoke thought and conversation. . . . I try to make them so they're not passive, so you're not just looking at the pages. You have to think and maybe come up with something else. A lot of times there are other things to observe or discover that are not apparent at first" (Allison 145). It is noteworthy that many of her books for children, even though published a good thirty years ago, are still in print. Noteworthy, too, is the recognition she earned as a photographer separate from her work as a children's book author. In recognition of her passing, the American Society of Media Photographers said about Hoban: "Her contributions to photography and to children's publishing will continue to inspire others—adults and children alike—to open their eyes to the world around them" (Blankstein 33). A walk through this collection reveals nothing less than pure inspiration.

—*Allison G. Kaplan*

Syd Hoff Papers

An early contributor to the de Grummond Collection, Syd Hoff, born Sydney Hoffberg (1912–2004), was one of the most prominent gag cartoonists and children's book authors. He achieved a tremendous level of success in a multitude of genres throughout his lifetime. In 1930, at age eighteen, he sold his first cartoon to the *New Yorker*—an event marking the start of a career that spanned over six decades and included thousands of cartoons for many mainstream publications, including the *Saturday Evening Post*, *Collier's*, *Esquire*, and *Playboy*. During the 1930s he cartooned for left-wing publications the *Daily Worker* and *New Masses*. Success was also achieved with advertising commissions for iconic companies such as Jell-O, Eveready Batteries, and General Electric. He had a TV show in 1947 called *Tales of Hoff* and wrote short stories for Alfred Hitchcock, Ellery Queen, and Charlie Chan—intended for adult readers. As a children's author, he wrote and/or illustrated over a hundred books including the beloved classic *Danny and the Dinosaur* (1958) and *Sammy the Seal* (1959), both for the I Can Read! series published by HarperCollins, as well as tutorials for future generations of cartoonists and illustrators.

As a cartoonist and illustrator, Hoff's work was easily recognizable. Bold and simple lines, coupled with whimsical, yet identifiable characters were the hallmarks of a style that remained unchanged throughout his career. He was able to depict the struggles of everyday life and an individual's ability to triumph without crossing the lines of decency. "Even in tough times, everyone is waiting to be amused, to laugh, to smile," Hoff once said. "A good cartoon has got to remind people of something they're faced with. They won't laugh unless it's something they've seen or experienced" (Fichtner 1B).

As in all his books thereafter, he demonstrated an ability to pique the curiosity and imagination of children—and encourage reading at an early age. Themes of friendship, kindness, inclusion, and fairness are common threads in his children's books, along with likable and clever boys and girls. His stories often feature gentle animal characters, eager for a break from their normal routine in search of adventure and interaction with children and adults, yet always returning home where they normally belong by the end of the day. Plots are uncomplicated and the artistic style is simple, yet amusing. "I like to make kids laugh. . . . A lot of people think it's easy to write for children, but children are critical and have their own requirements. . . . These children will know almost immediately whether a book is 'real' or not. It can be fantasy, but it must be believable," Hoff once said (Flor 406).

Syd Hoff passed away in 2004, leaving a legacy that spans over six decades and includes genres for both children and adults. He had the ability to effect change on an individual and collective level, and he welcomed the early reader into a world of imagination and adventure.

—*Carol Edmonston*

Tasha Tudor Papers

The American illustrator and author Tasha Tudor painted New England scenes that inspired people around the world to envy life in New England. She wrote and painted as Tasha Tudor but was born Starling Burgess in Boston, Massachusetts, in 1915. Her father, W. Starling Burgess, pioneered pontoon aircraft and designed yachts that won America's Cup races. Her mother, Rosamond Tudor, painted portraits under her maiden name.

Young Tasha was sent to live with the family of one of Nathaniel Hawthorne's granddaughters in Redding, Connecticut, after her parents divorced. While there she met and married Thomas L. McCready Jr. in 1938. Her first book, *Pumpkin Moonshine*, was published the same year. The McCreadys started their family in Redding, but moved to New Hampshire in 1945. After Tasha and McCready divorced, she and her four children legally changed their names to Tudor. From 1972 until her death in 2008, Tudor lived on a remote farm in Marlborough, Vermont.

Tudor authored or illustrated approximately a hundred books and painted fourteen hundred Christmas cards over a seventy-year career. Although principally known for her illustrations, she was also a noted gardener, weaver, doll-maker, and watercolorist. She collected four hundred pieces of antique clothing, which she wore and used as models for her paintings.

The Tasha Tudor Papers comprise contributions from several different sources, beginning with Tudor herself. Tasha Tudor contributed two paintings from *First Delights* (1966) and materials for *Tasha Tudor's Favorite Christmas Carols* (1978): typescript, galleys, proofs, color separations, layouts, and blues. Her Rand McNally editor, Dorothy Haas, contributed correspondence concerning four of Tudor's books and three Advent calendars. The Wm John and Priscilla T. Hare Collection (3,063 items) consists largely of print materials and related ephemera acquired during the compilation of the Hares' bibliography *Tasha Tudor: The Direction of Her Dreams* (1998). The Collection also documents the books of her husband, Thomas L. McCready Jr., and her two daughters, Bethany Tudor and Efner Holmes. The Hare Collection attempts to preserve every printing of every book and dust jacket Tasha Tudor wrote and/or illustrated, including paperback copies. Many pieces are inscribed by Tudor to specific people, some with extra drawings. The result is a comprehensive collection of art in various media related to Tasha Tudor's life and work.

—*Wm John Hare*

All the young Richard Peck thought of growing up in Decatur, Illinois, was moving to New York and becoming a novelist. And, eventually, he did, although it was not until he was in his late thirties and unemployed (but in New York) that he wrote his first work of fiction, which would eventually become his first novel, *Don't Look and It Won't Hurt*, published in 1972.

And where was that novel, written by the quintessential adopted New Yorker, set? Back in the Midwest, as would be so many of Peck's acclaimed novels, from his fantasy-tinged Blossom Culp books, to such YA classics as *Remembering the Good Times* (1985), to his Scott O'Dell Award–winning *The River Between Us* (2003), to his 2000 Newbery Medal–winning *A Year Down Yonder* (2000). One is reminded of Allen Say's comment in *Grandfather's Journey* about his move from Japan to the United States, "The funny thing is, the moment I am in one country, I am homesick for the other." The de Grummond Collection contains notes and manuscripts for all of these works.

In an era in which an allegiance to "kid-speak" held sway in realism, Peck's voice was always inimitably his own: stern, sentimental, epigrammatic. In YA literature, which was always scrubbing itself of at least apparent didacticism, Peck stood alone in his refusal to give up or disguise his pulpit. He got away with it because he made us want to listen. Perhaps that stint in the army ghostwriting Sunday sermons for his base chaplain in the 1950s paid off.

Peck maintained a career as both a writer for children and one for teenagers (with four novels for adults as well) until the late 1990s when the success of the Grandma Dowdel books, beginning with *A Long Way from Chicago* (1998), as well as changes in YA publishing, led him to publish almost exclusively historical fiction for middle-grade readers (and two novels about anthropomorphized mice) from then on. These books for younger readers were gentler than Peck's teen novels but shared with them his signature themes: the need to stand up for what's right, the resistance to peer pressure, the value of role models, and the wisdom of the old. It's clear why Peck's middle-grade novels also had an established fan base among senior citizens, who perhaps saw in Uncle Miles Armsworth and Grandma Dowdel role models for speaking freely, damn the consequences.

Published in 2016, Richard Peck's last novel, *The Best Man*, was, in retrospect anyway, a valedictory. It was a middle-grade comedy, aimed at those same-aged readers he had been cultivating for the past twenty years, but, like his YA novels of the 1970s and 1980s, it was set in (very) contemporary times about (very) contemporary issues, involving in part the reactions of its young narrator, Archer, to his beloved uncle Paul's romance with (and, spoiler alert, marriage to) Archer's student teacher, the very role-modeling (and dishy) Mr. McLeod. And when the book came out, so did Peck, who publicly acknowledged his homosexuality for the first time at the age of eighty-two. The book did everything Peck's books do: it was funny, it made you cry, it made you think, it had a great old lady. It was signing off with a flourish.

The de Grummond Collection is home to the Richard Peck Papers, the largest collection of Peck's manuscripts, correspondence, essays, photographs, and other documents related to his life and work donated to the Collection between 1972 and his death in 2018, including the manuscript of his final novel.

—*Roger Sutton*

The James Marshall Collection

James Marshall was born in San Antonio, Texas, and spent his early years on a farm. He was quite an accomplished violist and even won a scholarship to study at the New England Conservatory as a young man. However, a freak accident affected his hand and forced him to turn his attention to other pursuits. Unlike many of his contemporaries, Marshall did not attend art school, choosing instead to obtain his degree in French and history. He taught high school French and Spanish in Boston for two years, from 1968 to 1970, while he drew in his spare time. A publishing friend who saw his sketches contacted someone at Houghton Mifflin about him and set up an interview. The next day, Marshall had his first assignment—illustrating *Plink, Plink, Plink* (1971) for author Byrd Baylor.

Marshall's simple lines and cartoonish style coupled with the amusing expressions of his characters make his work unique. In fact, it is often the unspoken wit and circumstance of the characters on the page that make his work so humorous. It is easy to see the artist's personal wit and humor reflected in his work.

His famous George and Martha series debuted the next year with *George and Martha* (1972) and was soon followed by six more volumes from 1973 to 1988. In 1974 Marshall created the best-selling and often banned series, The Stupids, with author Harry Allard, which ran until 1989. Frequent collaborators, he and Allard also developed the Miss Nelson books, which were quite popular as well. Another popular series of Marshall's was his Fox series, which he wrote under the pseudonym Edward Marshall. Published mostly during the 1980s, the series debuted in 1981, with the last book, *Fox on Stage* (1993), being released posthumously.

The James Marshall Papers first came to the de Grummond Collection in 1985, with the last donation received from the Marshall Estate shortly after his tragic death from a brain tumor in 1992. The collection consists of manuscripts, sketches, correspondence, proofs, galleys, and finished art for more than forty of his published titles. In addition, the de Grummond houses sketches and illustrations for approximately eighteen unpublished works. Despite this wealth of material, perhaps the real jewels in the Marshall archive are the thirty-one sketchbooks, which cover a myriad of topics and are full of illustrations for Marshall's greatest hits in their early stages. Marshall himself remarked on the value of these sketchbooks in a letter to former de Grummond curator Dee Jones in 1987: "I feel that sketchbooks are, by far, more interesting than finished art" (Letter [8 June]). It is obvious from additional correspondence that it was very important for James Marshall to provide his preparatory materials in order to show what is involved in his creative process. In a letter to Jones in March 1987 he said, "I'd like to donate a book from start to finish—sketchbooks, pencil sketches, color sketches, finishes, proofs, the works" (Letter [27 March]). Researchers reap the rewards of his generosity to de Grummond by being able to examine firsthand the genius that is James Marshall.

—*Danielle Bishop Stoulig*

A view of the book stacks. Photograph by Kelly Dunn.

The de Grummond's collection of G. A. Henty. Photograph by Kelly Dunn.

Another view of the stacks.
Photograph by Kelly Dunn.

Dolls keep watch over manuscript boxes. Photograph by
Kelly Dunn.

A view of the manuscript collection. Photograph by Kelly Dunn.

original drawing for
Curious George. N.7. – Paris, Spring 1940

To Lena Y. de Grummond
with best wishes – H. a. Rey – May 1972

An original illustration of Curious George and the Man in the Yellow Hat, by H. A. Rey, sent to
Lena de Grummond in 1970. Courtesy of the de Grummond Collection.

Original art from *Hazel's Amazing Mother* (1985), written and illustrated by Rosemary Wells.
Courtesy of the de Grummond Collection.

First University of Southern Mississippi Children's Literature Medallion, awarded to Lois Lenski in 1969. Courtesy of the de Grummond Collection.

The back of Lenski's medallion with an engraving of her image. Courtesy of the de Grummond Collection.

Photograph of E. H. Shepard holding the University of Southern Mississippi Children's Literature Medallion, delivered to him in 1970 by Lena de Grummond. Courtesy of the de Grummond Collection.

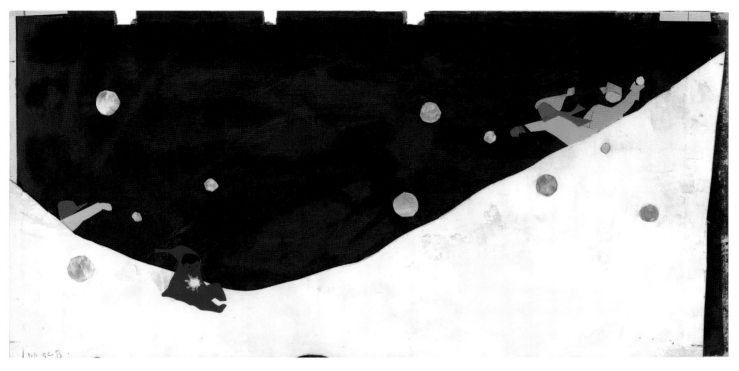

An original illustration from *The Snowy Day* (1962), written and illustrated by Ezra Jack Keats.
Courtesy of the de Grummond Collection.

The Caldecott Medal Awarded to Ezra Jack Keats in 1963. Courtesy of the de Grummond Collection.

the children's literature association

Newsletter

April, 1974

Dear ChLA Member:

The last several months have been busy ones for The Children's Literature Association. In addition to memberships which must be processed, the Association held its first annual conference March 15 - 17 at the University of Connecticut, Storrs, Ct. Despite the problems that a first conference is subject to, it was successful for a number of reason, foremost being the degree of communication established among those attending.

Those of us in children's literature seek new ideas and a forum in which these ideas can be exchanged. The conference provided this and lessened the sense of isolation teachers of children's literature too often have. I would like to thank those of you who attended for establishing this communication, and hope that future conferences will continue to be places where ideas can be communicated.

March 16th of the conference, a general membership meeting was held where a number of very important issues were raised. Perhaps the most important was the question of the Association bylaws. A request was made that copies of the bylaws be made available to the general membership. At the Executive Board Meeting following the conference this issue was discussed and its importance again agreed upon. The bylaws will be a bit slow going out, however, as the Board voted to insert clauses to provide openings on the Board, to be filled by nomination and vote of the membership; and to provide a greater opportunity for participation of the membership in decision making.

The question of regional associations was a second issue discussed at the membership meeting. In response to opinions from the membership, it was decided to postpone the formation of regional associations for at least a year, to enable the national Association is be built up more and solidify the organization.

The Executive Board Meeting was held Sunday afternoon after the finish of the conference. Three issues were discussed at length: membership fees; the establishing of a ChLA Book Award; and the bylaws. The Board voted to raise membership fees due to increased costs in mailing and printing. It was also decided to coincide the membership and fiscal years due to the date of publication of the journal. The membership year will run from May 1 to May1, as does the fiscal year. The new membership fees, effective May 1, 1974, will be: $7.50, student membership; $14.50, regular membership; $22.00, institutional membership.

With the membership year changed from August to May, members who enrolled in the Association during the period from August, 1973 to March, 1974, will be receiving renewal forms for 1974 sometime during the month of May. 1974 membership will include the cost of a copy of Volume III of the journal, Children's Literature: The Great Excluded, which will be available May 1, 1974. We apologize for any confusion there might be in this change-over process. The Association being less than a year old, it is still in the process of arranging fiscal years and memberships. If you have questions on this matter, please write to me.

the 1974 children's literature association annual conference

"Cultural and Critical Values in Children's Literature"

march 15 - 17

The program from the first Children's Literature Association Conference in 1974. The de Grummond Collection is home to the ChLA archives. Courtesy of the de Grummond Collection.

The April 1974 ChLA Newsletter, with update from Executive Secretary Anne Devereaux Jordan on the first annual conference. Courtesy of the de Grummond Collection.

things we've got to have, we're going to make our own beds and a table and some benches, the only nice thing down here is our fire place and big fire and log house I love them but dont like

ARK CAN SAW

A page from Amelia's diary, kept by a ten-year-old girl who traveled by covered wagon from Iowa to Arkansas in 1895. Courtesy of the de Grummond Collection.

The unnamed "Circus Mural," created for the de Grummond Children's Literature Collection by Esphyr Slobodkina and completed in 1970. Photograph by Kelly Dunn.

Original art from *Trapped! A Whale's Rescue* (2015), written by Robert Burleigh and illustrated by Wendell Minor. Courtesy of the de Grummond Collection.

Tana Hoban at work in an undated photograph. Courtesy of the de Grummond Collection.

A contact sheet of photographs of children on a playground taken by Tana Hoban. Courtesy of the de Grummond Collection.

Original illustration from *Henrietta Lays Some Eggs* (1977) by Syd Hoff. Courtesy of the de Grummond Collection.

Original Syd Hoff cartoons from "Laugh It Off," King Features Syndicate. Courtesy of the de Grummond Collection.

Painting by Tasha Tudor commissioned by President Ronald Reagan for the White House Easter Egg Roll.
Courtesy of the de Grummond Collection.

Photograph of Richard Peck. Courtesy of Sonya Sones.

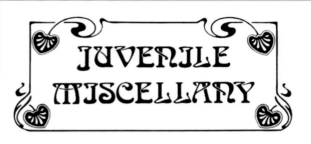

de Grummond Children's
Literature Research Collection
The University of
Southern Mississippi

Spring, 1991
Volume 21
Number 1

Richard Peck Awarded Medallion
At 24th Annual Children's Book Festival

Richard Peck
Author

Photo By: Don Lewis

The twenty-fourth annual Children's Book Festival of the University of Southern Mississippi was held on the Hattiesburg campus March 6-8. Author Richard Peck was the recipient of the University's Medallion given to an author or illustrator for their distinguished contribution to children's literature. Peck, author of more than 30 books, is renowned for his young adult titles, such as REMEMBERING THE

GOOD TIMES, ARE YOU IN THE HOUSE ALONE?, and GHOSTS I HAVE BEEN. In 1990 he won the School Library Journal/ Young Adult Services Division Author Achievement Award. His latest novels are THOSE SUMMER GIRLS I NEVER MET and VOICES AFTER MIDNIGHT. Other featured guests included Aliki, James Rice, Dorothy Butler, Brian and Valerie Alderson, Joan Atkinson, Patsy Perritt, Drs. Martin and Lillie Pope, and Jay Stailey.

Special events included a Storytelling Evening at Cabot Lodge, book and medallion sales, autograph sessions, author luncheons, the "Image of the Child," a special exhibition from the de Grummond Collection commemorating its twenty-fifth anniversary, a reception and award banquet, critiques of the 1991 Newbery-Caldecott Medal winners, and the Ezra Jack Keats Lecture and Luncheon.

A standing ovation met Richard Peck's forceful acceptance speech for the USM Medallion at the award banquet. Citing the University as a national center for books and young readers, Peck conveyed his appreciation for the Medallion, claiming that it was "too meaningful not to share." He explained, "I share it with a long-ago Latin teacher who set me on the path that lead me here, and I share it with a young girl I will never meet—a girl who was shamed by her mother." Peck decried the harm that a religious fundamentalist woman had wreaked on her vulnerable teenage daughter by her attempt to ban his book THE GHOST BELONGED TO ME. He pointed out that he censors his own books as he writes and responded to the mother's complaints by declaring that "books aren't that powerful, and your children are not that innocent." He maintains that only a "willing minority" of students read at all today.

Peck views the rise in religious fundamentalist book banning as part of a political cause masked as a religious one, targeting books and libraries. These activities find literate, middle-class parents because they fear the loss of control over their children. He acknowledged that teachers, librarians, authors, and responsible parents "fear for the safety of ignorant children ... fear for children who would prefer a car to a high school education and have proved it ... fear for the kids sitting out on their hoods in the mall parking lot because

(continued next page)

Issue of *Juvenile Miscellany* announcing Peck as winner of the Children's Literature Medallion.
Courtesy of the de Grummond Collection.

ACKNOWLEDGMENTS

We would like to thank Elizabeth La Beaud and Leah Rials for the digitization of many images in this book. Danielle Bishop Stoulig, former assistant curator of the de Grummond Collection; Brooke Cruthirds, current assistant curator; de Grummond Collection specialist Amanda McRaney; and Claire Thompson, coordinator for the Ezra Jack Keats Award, provided crucial aid on the project. Karlie Herndon and Matthew Fillingame assisted us with locating and selecting images. Lorraine Stuart, curator of archives and manuscripts and head of special collections at the University of Southern Mississippi, was also a great help and support. Thanks also to Lisa Jones and Virginia Butler, who offered assistance, and to university photographer Kelly Dunn, who took lovely pictures for us.

Eric Tribunella also thanks his spouse, Jerrid Boyette, for his support and partnership. The invaluable assistance of Elizabeth Hughes, assistant to the dean for academic affairs and operations in the College of Arts and Sciences, made it possible to find additional time to work on this project.

We want to thank the staff at the University Press of Mississippi for their enthusiastic support and patience. The project would not have been possible without Craig Gill, Katie Keene, Mary Heath, Pete Halverson, Valerie Jones, and Anne Stascavage.

Finally, we want to acknowledge Onva K. Boshears, former dean of library science, and Aubrey K. Lucas, former president of the University of Southern Mississippi, for their longstanding commitment to the de Grummond Collection.

TIMELINE

Lena de Grummond Children's Literature Collection and Fay B. Kaigler Children's Book Festival

1965 — Lena de Grummond begins teaching children's literature at the University of Southern Mississippi.

1966 — Lena de Grummond begins her letter-writing campaign, asking authors and illustrators to send materials to use in her classes.

1968 — Conference on the Writing, Illustrating, and Publishing of Children's Books is held at the University of Southern Mississippi. This conference was the vision of Dr. Warren Tracy, chairman of the Library Science Department, and Dr. William D. McCain, president of the university, as a way to highlight and announce the children's literature collection that Lena de Grummond had built over the previous two years.

1969 — The conference is renamed the "Children's Book Festival" and includes an event that has become "an honored tradition—presentation of the University of Southern Mississippi Medallion, an award for distinguished service in the field of children's literature."

1970 — The Children's Book Collection is officially named the "Lena Y. de Grummond Collection."

1977–1980 — Dr. Onva K. Boshears serves as director of the Children's Book Festival.

1980	Ezra Jack Keats receives the University of Southern Mississippi Medallion. Following the award, Keats becomes one of the strongest supporters of the Children's Book Festival and the de Grummond Collection.
1980–1994	Dr. Jeannine Laughlin-Porter serves as director of the Children's Book Festival.
1985	The Keats Foundation establishes an Ezra Jack Keats lectureship at the Children's Book Festival. Brian Alderson serves as the first Keats lecturer.
1994–2001	Dr. Boshears resumes directorship of the Children's Book Festival.
2001	The Children's Book Festival is renamed Fay B. Kaigler Children's Book Festival in honor of Fay B. Kaigler, a retired elementary school teacher from Mississippi, who contributed a planned gift to the festival. Like Lena de Grummond, Fay Kaigler was a graduate of Louisiana State University. According to the article "The History of the Fay B. Kaigler Children's Book Festival," Kaigler's gift "to the university will continue the festival's tradition of encouraging writers to strive for excellence in children's literature and of providing information to teachers and librarians."
2002–2004	Dr. Rosemary Chance serves as director of the Fay B. Kaigler Children's Book Festival.
2004–2010	Dr. Catharine Bomhold serves as director of the Fay B. Kaigler Children's Book Festival.
2007–	Karen Rowell serves as coordinator of Fay B. Kaigler Children's Book Festival.

The University of Southern Mississippi Medallion Winners

The University of Southern Mississippi Medallion is an award for distinguished service in the field of children's literature. A committee of professionals associated with children's literature selects the recipient each year. Unique among literary prizes, the medallion is awarded for an individual's total body of work, rather than for one particular work, and each medallion is different. Cast in silver for the recipient and for permanent display in the de Grummond Collection and in bronze for wider distribution, a profile of the honoree is engraved on the face, or obverse, of the medallion, and an illustration from the honoree's work is engraved on the reverse side. Since the first award to author Lois Lenski at the Second Annual Children's Book Festival, the medallion has been presented to an outstanding array of children's authors and illustrators.

—from "History of the Fay B. Kaigler Children's Book Festival," University of Southern Mississippi

1969: Lois Lenski
1970: Ernest H. Shepard
1971: Roger Duvoisin
1972: Marcia Brown
1973: Lynd Ward
1974: Taro Yashima
1975: Barbara Cooney
1976: Scott O'Dell
1977: Adrienne Adams
1978: Madeleine L'Engle
1979: Leonard Everett Fisher
1980: Ezra Jack Keats
1981: Maurice Sendak
1982: Beverly Cleary
1983: Katherine Paterson
1984: Peter Spier
1985: Arnold Lobel
1986: Jean Craighead George
1987: Paula Fox
1988: Jean Fritz
1989: Lee Bennett Hopkins
1990: Charlotte Zolotow
1991: Richard Peck
1992: James Marshall
1993: Quentin Blake
1994: Ashley Bryan

1995: Tomie dePaola
1996: Patricia MacLachlan
1997: Eric Carle
1998: Elaine Konigsburg
1999: Russell Freedman
2000: David Macaulay
2001: Virginia Hamilton
2002: Rosemary Wells
2003: Lois Lowry
2004: Jerry Pinkney
2005: Kevin Henkes
2006: Walter Dean Myers
2007: Eve Bunting
2008: Pat Mora
2009: Judy Blume
2010: David Wiesner
2011: T. A. Barron
2012: Jane Yolen
2013: Jon Scieszka
2014: Christopher Paul Curtis
2015: Paul O. Zelinsky
2016: Jacqueline Woodson
2017: Kate DiCamillo
2018: Dav Pilkey
2019: Tamora Pierce
2020: Rita Williams-Garcia

THE EZRA JACK KEATS BOOK AWARDS

Deborah Pope

In 2012 the Ezra Jack Keats Foundation marked the fiftieth anniversary of the printing of Keats's beloved classic, *The Snowy Day*, and it was the year the Ezra Jack Keats Award moved from the New York Public Library (NYPL) to the de Grummond Children's Literature Collection, one of the foremost collections in the United States and the home of the Keats Archive.

The Ezra Jack Keats Award was initiated in 1986 by Hannah Nuber, a librarian at the New York Public Library, as a partnership between the EJK Foundation and the NYPL. Herself a survivor of the Holocaust, Nuber had created the Early Childhood Reading and Information Collection (ECRIC), a reading room devoted to bringing the most up-to-date parenting information and progressive children's literature to the new parents served by her NYPL branch in Greenwich Village. Hannah understood the need for more diverse literature for young children to build their self-esteem and, more importantly, their empathy and tolerance for others. The great success of ECRIC sparked the idea of a children's book award that would encourage new authors and illustrators to make books like those created by Ezra Jack Keats.

As the years went by, the Foundation's relationship with the de Grummond deepened through the creation of the Keats Fellowship, the Keats Archive, and the Keats Lecture and Luncheon at the Children's Book Festival. The multiple connections between the EJK Foundation and the de Grummond made it clear that the future of the award could flourish here as well, so the management of the awards transferred from the NYPL to the de Grummond. In Hattiesburg, Honor Books were added as a category, allowing the award to bring recognition to even more artists early in their careers. Since 2012 alone the EJK Award has recognized the talent of Meg Medina, Don Tate, Ryan T. Higgins, Misty Copeland, Christian Robinson, and Derek Barnes, to name a few. An overwhelming number of EJK Award winners and honorees have gone on to win many awards, including the Caldecott and Newbery.

With the de Grummond as the administering institution, the EJK Award has attracted premiere professionals working in the field of children's literature from across the country to serve on the EJK Award committee. Our jury members are often the same people who serve on the Caldecott, Newbery, Coretta Scott King, and Pura Belpré committees. What distinguishes the EJK Award committee from all the other children's book award committees is that EJK's includes authors and illustrators, making the award one judged by peers, as well as scholars and librarians. Perhaps most importantly, the EJK Award is unique among virtually all children's book awards in that it supports and promotes diversity in children's literature without focusing on any one group. The result is that EJK Awards have honored books about African American, Chinese, Korean, Japanese, Tanzanian, and Hispanic children, among others, and have focused on subjects ranging from tea parties to first days of school, slavery to aging grandparents, bullying to prejudice, and flying witches to hibernating bears. In a sense the EJK Award winner and honor list includes the range of books we aim for when we decide to build a diverse library.

BIBLIOGRAPHY

CHAPTER 1: LENA DE GRUMMOND AND THE FOUNDING OF THE COLLECTION

Arnold, Yvonne. "Lena Young de Grummond: Woman with a Dream." *The Talon: Lena Y. de Grummond Commemorative Issue*. Southern Miss Alumni Association. Spring 2016, pp. 4–6.

"Biographical Sketch." Lena de Grummond and Lynn Delaune Papers, de Grummond Children's Literature Collection, University of Southern Mississippi, Hattiesburg.

"Biographical Sketch." Mina and H. Arthur Klein Papers, de Grummond Children's Literature Collection, University of Southern Mississippi, Hattiesburg.

de Grummond, Lena Y. "Growth of an Idea: The de Grummond Collection." de Grummond Children's Literature Collection, University of Southern Mississippi, Hattiesburg.

de Grummond, Lena. Letter to Laszlo Matulay. May 18, 1966. Lena de Grummond and Lynn Delaune Papers, de Grummond Children's Literature Collection, University of Southern Mississippi, Hattiesburg.

de Grummond, Lena. Notebooks, 1966-1970, Lena de Grummond and Lynn Delaune Papers, de Grummond Children's Literature Collection, University of Southern Mississippi, Hattiesburg.

"Dr. Lena Young de Grummond Receives Exchange Club's Golden Deeds Award." *Franklin Banner*, May 24, 1984. n.p.

"First USM Library Medal Presented to Lois Lenski." *Clarion-Ledger / Jackson Daily News*, 23 March 1969.

Hader, Berta, and Elmer Hader. Letter to Lena de Grummond, 28 January 1966, Berta and Elmer Hader Papers, de Grummond Children's Literature Collection, University of Southern Mississippi, Hattiesburg.

Hader, Berta, and Elmer Hader. Letter to Lena de Grummond, 14 March 1966, Berta and Elmer Hader Papers, de Grummond Children's Literature Collection, University of Southern Mississippi, Hattiesburg.

Hill, Margaret Ohler. Letter to Lena de Grummond, 8 June 1968, de Grummond Children's Literature Collection, University of Southern Mississippi, Hattiesburg.

"History of the Fay B. Kaigler Children's Book Festival." University of Southern Mississippi. https://www.usm.edu/childrens-book-festival/history-fay-b-kaigler-childrens-book-festival.

Hoff, Syd. Letter to Children's Literature Collection, 11 November 1967, Syd Hoff Papers, de Grummond Children's Literature Collection, University of Southern Mississippi, Hattiesburg.

Holl, Adelaide. Letter to Lena de Grummond, 10 June 1968, de Grummond Children's Literature Collection, University of Southern Mississippi, Hattiesburg.

Johnson, Lois S. Letter to Lena de Grummond, 3 August 1966, de Grummond Children's Literature Collection, University of Southern Mississippi, Hattiesburg.

Klein, H. Arthur. Letter to Lena de Grummond, 3 January 1966, Mina and H. Arthur Klein Papers, de Grummond Children's Literature Collection, University of Southern Mississippi, Hattiesburg.

Lambou, Madeline. "The Midas Touch of Lena de Grummond." *The Pen Woman*. December 1969, p. 7.

Leeper, Clair d'Artois. "The Bibliophiles of the de Grummond." *Louisiana State Alumni News*, April 1971, pp. 13–14.

L'Engle, Madeleine. Letter to Lena de Grummond, 24 October 1966, Madeleine L'Engle Papers, de Grummond Children's Literature Collection, University of Southern Mississippi, Hattiesburg.

L'Engle, Madeleine. Letter to Miss Rosenbaum, 13 July 1968, Madeleine L'Engle Papers, de Grummond Children's Literature Collection, University of Southern Mississippi, Hattiesburg.

Lenski, Lois. Letter to Lena de Grummond, 6 May 1966, Lois Lenski Papers, de Grummond Children's Literature Collection, University of Southern Mississippi, Hattiesburg.

Lundin, Anne. "A Dukedom Large Enough: The de Grummond Collection." *The Lion and the Unicorn*, vol. 22, no. 3, September 1998, pp. 303–11.

Murphy, Emily. "Unpacking the Archive: Value, Pricing, and the Letter-Writing Campaign of Dr. Lena Y. de Grummond." *Children's Literature Association Quarterly*, vol. 39, no. 4, 2014, pp. 551–68.

Orlob, Helen. Letter to Lena de Grummond, 30 October 1967, de Grummond Children's Literature Collection, University of Southern Mississippi, Hattiesburg.

Rey, H. A. Letter to Lena de Grummond, 20 April 1966, H. A. and Margret Rey Papers, de Grummond Children's Literature Collection, University of Southern Mississippi, Hattiesburg.

"Scope and Content." Lena de Grummond and Lynn Delaune Papers, de Grummond Children's Literature Collection, University of Southern Mississippi, Hattiesburg.

Tolkien, J. R. R. Letter to Lena de Grummond, 15 August 1966, de Grummond Children's Literature Collection, University of Southern Mississippi, Hattiesburg.

Tolkien, J. R. R. Letter to Lena de Grummond, 17 October 1966, de Grummond Children's Literature Collection, University of Southern Mississippi, Hattiesburg.

Warner, Gertrude. Letter to Lena de Grummond, 4 January 1968, Gertrude Warner Papers, de Grummond Children's Literature Collection, University of Southern Mississippi, Hattiesburg.

Williams, Garth. Letter to Lena de Grummond, 1 March 1966, de Grummond Children's Literature Collection, University of Southern Mississippi, Hattiesburg.

Bottigheimer, Ruth B. "*Fairy Godfather*, Fairy-Tale History, and Fairy-Tale Scholarship: A Response to Dan Ben-Amos, Jan M. Ziolkowski, and Francisco Vaz da Silva." *Journal of American Folklore*, vol. 123, no. 490, Fall 2010, pp. 447–96.

Bottigheimer, Ruth B. *Fairy Tales: A New History*. SUNY Press, 2009.

Bottigheimer, Ruth B. "Upward and Outward: Fairy Tales and Popular, Print, and Proletarian Culture." *Elore*, vol. 17, no. 2, 2010, pp. 104–20.

Schenda, Rudolf. "Semiliterate and Semi-Oral Processes." Translated by Ruth B. Bottigheimer. *Marvels and Tales* vol. 21, no. 1, 2007, pp. 127–40.

Sumpter, Caroline. *The Victorian Press and the Fairy Tale*. Palgrave, 2008.

Tomkowiak, Ingrid. *Lesebuchgeschichten: Erzählstoff in Schullesebüchern, 1770–1920*. W. de Gruyter, 1993.

Uther, Hans-Jörg. *The Type of International Folktales. A Classification and Bibliography*. 2 vols. Academia Scientarum Fennica, 2004.

CHAPTER 4: READERS AND PRIMERS

Cohen, Daniel. "The Origin and Development of the *New England Primer*." *Children's Literature*, vol. 5, 1976, pp. 52–57.

Kammen, Carol. "The McGuffey *Readers*." *Children's Literature* vol. 5, 1976, pp. 58–63.

McGuffey's First Eclectic Reader. New York, American Book Company, 1896.

The New-England Primer: Improved for the More Easy Attaining the True Reading of English. To Which Is Added the Assembly of Divines' Catechism. Middletown, CT, Clark and Lyman, for Thomas Spencer, Jr., 1820.

The Royal Primer. London, Printed for J. Newbery, circa 1760.

Sanders, Charles W. *Sanders' Union Reader. Number One. For Primary Schools and Families*. 1861. New York, Ivison, Blakeman, Taylor & Co., 1877.

The Southern Primer, or, Child's First Lessons in Spelling and Reading. Richmond, Adolphus Morris, 1860.

Zipes, Jack, Lissa Paul, Lynne Vallone, Peter Hunt, and Gillian Avery. "Primers and Readers." *The Norton Anthology of Children's Literature*, edited by Jack Zipes, Lissa Paul, Lynne Vallone, Peter Hunt, and Gillian Avery, Norton, 2005, pp. 75–86.

CHAPTER 5: THE GOLDEN AGE OF ILLUSTRATED CHILDREN'S BOOKS

Blackburn, Henry. *Randolph Caldecott: A Personal Memoir of His Early Art Career*. 1886. London, Sampson, Low, Marston, Searly, and Rivington, 1892.

Crane, Walter. *The Baby's Opera*. London, Frederick Warne and Co., 1877.

Crane, Walter. *Of the Decorative Illustration of Books Old and New*. 1896. Brachen Books, 1984.

Golden, Catherine. *Serials to Graphic Novels: The Evolution of the Victorian Illustrated Book*. University Press of Florida, 2017.

Greenaway, Kate. *Under the Window*. New York, Frederick Warne and Co., 1879.

Lawson, Robert. "Howard Pyle and His Times." *Illustrators of Children's Books, 1744–1945*, compiled by Bertha E. Mahony, Louise Payson Latimer, and Beulah Folmsbee, Horn Book, 1970, pp. 107–34.

Lundin, Anne. "Kate Greenaway's Critical and Commercial Reception." *Princeton University Library Chronicle*, vol. 57, no. 1, 1995, pp. 127–46.

Sendak, Maurice. *Caldecott & Co.: Notes on Books and Pictures*. Farrar, Straus and Giroux, 1988.

Chapter 6: Children's Series Fiction

Avery, Gillian. "'Remarkable and Winning': A Hundred Years of American Heroines." *The Lion and the Unicorn*, vol. 13, no. 1, 1989, pp. 7–20.

Johnson, Deidre. "Nancy Drew—A Modern Elsie Dinsmore?" *The Lion and the Unicorn*, vol. 18, no. 1, 1994, pp. 13–24.

MacLeod, Anne Scott. *American Childhood: Essays on Children's Literature of the Nineteenth and Twentieth Centuries*. University of Georgia Press, 1994.

Chapter 7: Editions and Variants

Adoff, Arnold. *black is brown is tan*. 1973. Illustrated by Emily Arnold McCully, HarperCollins, 2002.

Alcott, Louisa May. *Little Women*. 1868. Edited by Anne Hiebert Alton, Broadview Press, 2001.

Blume, Judy. *Are You There God? It's Me, Margaret*. 1970. Random House, 2014.

Comenius, Johannes Amos. *Orbis Sensualium Pictus: Hoc Est Omnium Principalium in Mundo Rerum, & in Vita Aeionum [Visible World: or, A Nomenclature, and Pictures, of all the Chief Things that are in the World, and of Men's Employments therein, 12th Edition]*. Translated by Charles Hoole, Leacroft, 1777.

Greetham, D. C. *Textual Scholarship: An Introduction*. Garland, 1994.

Lofting, Hugh. *The Story of Doctor Dolittle*. 1920. Yearling, 1988.

Otis, James. *Toby Tyler, or Ten Weeks with a Circus*. Harper and Brothers, 1881.

Otis, James. *Toby Tyler, or Ten Weeks with a Circus*. Edited by Grace Hogarth, Collins and Harvill Press, 1971.

Reed, W. Maxwell. *The Earth for Sam: The Story of Mountains, Rivers, Dinosaurs and Men*. Drawings by Karl Moseley, Harcourt, Brace & Co., 1930, Revised 1960.

Williams, William Proctor, and Craig S. Abbott. *An Introduction to Bibliographical and Textual Studies*. 2nd ed., MLA, 1989.

Zim, Herbert S. *The Universe*. 1961. Illustrated by Gustav Schrotter, Morrow, 1973.

Chapter 8: Nineteenth-Century Children's Magazines

Parris, Brandy. "Difficult Sympathy in the Reconstruction-Era Animal Stories of *Our Young Folks*." *Children's Literature*, vol. 31, 2003, pp. 25–49.

Ringel, Paul B. *Commercializing Childhood: Children's Magazines, Urban Gentility, and the Ideal of the Child Consumer in the United States, 1823–1918*. University of Massachusetts Press, 2015.

Weil, Lisa. "'A Good Line of Advertising': The Historical Development of Children's Advertising as Reflected in *St. Nicholas Magazine*, 1873–1905." 2007. University of Missouri–Columbia, MA Thesis.

Wright, Nazera Sadiq. "'Our Hope Is in the Rising Generation': Locating African American Children's Literature in the Children's Department of the *Colored American*." *Who Writes for Black Children? African American Children's Literature Before 1900*, edited by Anna Mae Duane and Katherine Capshaw, University of Minnesota Press, 2017, pp. 147–63.

CHAPTER 10: PICTURE BOOK ART

Bader, Barbara. *American Picturebooks: From Noah's Ark to the Beast Within*. Macmillan, 1976.

Sanders, Joe Sutliff. "Chaperoning Words: Meaning-Making in Comics and Picture Books." *Children's Literature*, vol. 41, 2013, pp. 57–90.

Sendak, Maurice. "Randolph Caldecott: An Appreciation." *The Randolph Caldecott Treasury*, selected and edited by Elizabeth T. Billington, Frederick Warne, 1978, pp. 21–25.

CHAPTER 11: CHILDREN'S NONFICTION

Ammon, Francesca Russello. "Unearthing *Benny the Bulldozer*: The Culture of Clearance in Postwar Children's Books." *Technology and Culture*, vol. 53, no. 2, 2012, pp. 306–36.

Barlow, Diane L. "Children, Books, and Biology." *BioScience*, vol. 41, no. 3, 1991, 166–68.

Bendick, Jeanne. *The First Book of Space Travel*. Rev. ed., F. Watts, 1953.

Cobb, Theo. *Vicki Cobb, The "Julia Child" of Kids' Hands-on Science*. www.vickicobb.com. Accessed 18 July 2018.

Giblin, James Cross. "More Than Just the Facts: A Hundred Years of Children's Nonfiction." *Horn Book Magazine*, vol. 76, July/August 2000, pp. 413–24, www.hbook.com/2013/04/creating-books/publishing/more-than-just-the-facts-a-hundred-years-of-childrens-nonfiction/. Accessed 19 July 19 2018.

Greene, Carla. *I Want to Be a Space Pilot*. Children's Press, 1961.

Hurd, Edith Thacher. *Benny the Bulldozer*. Lothrop, Lee and Amp, 1947.

Inness, Sherrie A. "'The Enchantment of Mixing Spoons': Cooking Lessons for Girls and Boys." *Kitchen Culture in America: Popular Representations of Food, Gender, and Race*, edited by Sherrie A. Inness, University of Pennsylvania Press, 2001, pp. 119–38.

Johnson, Constance. *When Mother Lets Us Cook: A Book of Simple Receipts for Little Folk*. Moffat, Yard, 1908.

Mickenberg, Julia L. *Learning from the Left: Children's Literature, the Cold War, and Radical Politics in the United States*. Oxford University Press, 2006.

Meltzer, Milton. "Where Do All the Prizes Go? The Face for Nonfiction." *Horn Book Magazine*, vol. 52, February 1976, pp. 18–21, www.hbook.com/1976/02/choosing-books/horn-book-magazine/where-do-all-the-prizes-go-the-case-for-nonfiction-2/#. Accessed 18 July 2018.

Pérez-Peña, Richard. "Herbert S. Zim Is Dead at 85; Wrote Children's Science Books." *New York Times*, Section B, Page 10, Column 1, 12 December 1994.

Riedel, Kari Ness. "12 Nonfiction Books Kids Will Actually Read." www.readbrightly.com/non fiction-books-kids-recommend/. Accessed July 17, 2018.

Wright, Marie T. "Augusta Stevenson and the Bobbs-Merrill Childhood of Famous Americans Biographies." *Indian Libraries*, vol. 2, no. 2, 1993, pp. 11–21.

Chapter 12: African American Children's Literature and Writers

Baker, Augusta. *Books about Negro Life for Children*. New York Public Library, 1963.

Baker, Augusta. "The Changing Image of the Black in Children's Literature." *Horn Book Magazine*, vol. 51, February 1975, pp. 79–88, https://www.hbook.com/1975/02/choosing-books/horn-book-magazine/the-changing-image-of-the-black-in-childrens-literature/.

Bontemps, Arna. *Sad-Faced Boy*. Houghton Mifflin, 1937.

Bontemps, Arna. *You Can't Pet a Possum*. William Morrow, 1934.

Bontemps, Arna, and Langston Hughes. *Popo and Fifina: Children of Haiti*. 1932. Macmillan, 1946.

Broderick, Dorothy. *Image of the Black in Children's Fiction*. Bowker, 1973.

Evans, Eva Knox. *Araminta*. Minton, Balch, and Co., 1935.

Evans, Eva Knox. *Jerome Anthony*. G. P. Putnam, 1936.

McNair, Jonda. "Reflections on Black Children's Literature: A Historical Perspective." *Horn Book Magazine*. 23 July 2018, https://www.hbook.com/2018/07/opinion/reflections-black-childrens-literature-historical-perspective/.

Rollins, Charlemae Hill. *Christmas Gif': An Anthology of Christmas Songs, Poems, and Stories Written by and about African Americans*. 1963. Morrow, 1993.

Rollins, Charlemae Hill. *We Build Together: A Reader's Guide to Negro Life and Literature for Elementary and High School Use*. National Council of Teachers of English, 1941.

Chapter 13: Southern Children's Literature

Bernstein, Robin. *Racial Innocence: Performing American Childhood from Slavery to Civil Rights*. New York University Press, 2011.

Connolly, Paula T. *Slavery in American Children's Literature, 1790–2010*. University of Iowa Press, 2013.

"Editorial." *The Children's Friend*, vol. 1, no. 12, 1863, p. 47.

Harris, Joel Chandler. *Little Mr. Thimblefinger and His Queer Country: What the Children Saw and Heard There*. Houghton, Mifflin, 1894.

Krementz, Jill. *Sweet Pea: A Black Girl Growing Up in the Rural South*. Harcourt, Brace and World, 1969.

Lyttle, Byrd. *Ellen Hunter: A Story of the War. Burke's Weekly for Boys and Girls*, vol. 1, no. 28–52, 1868.

MacCann, Donnarae. *White Supremacy in Children's Literature: Characterizations of African Americans, 1830–1900*. Garland Publishing, 1998.

West, Mark I. "Guest Editor's Introduction." *Southern Quarterly*, vol. 54, no. 3/4, 2017, pp. 5–9.

Chapter 14: Contemporary Children's and Young Adult Writers

Cart, Michael. *Young Adult Literature: From Romance to Realism*. 3rd ed., American Library Association, 2016.

Duyvis, Corrine. "Diverse Characters: Corinne Duyvis on the Decline of 'Issues' Books." *The Guardian*. https://www.theguardian.com/childrens-books-site/2014/oct/17/decline-of -issue-books-incidental-diversity. Accessed 20 October 2014.

Mercier, Cathryn M. "Realism." *Keywords for Children's Literature*, edited by Philip Nel and Lissa Paul. New York University Press, 2011, 198–201.

"The Official Nerdfighter Lexicon." *Nerdfighteria*. http://www.nerdfighteria.com/lexicon/. Accessed 14 January 2019.

"Publishing Statistics on Children's Books about People of Color and First/Native Nations and by People of Color and First/Native Nations Authors and Illustrators," *Cooperative Children's Book Center*, http://ccbc.education.wisc.edu/books/pcstats.asp. Accessed 24 May 2018.

Schwebel, Sara L. *Child-Sized History: Fictions of the Past in U.S. Classrooms*. Vanderbilt University Press, 2011.

Trites, Roberta Seelinger. *Twain, Alcott, and the Birth of the Adolescent Reform Novel*. University of Iowa, 2007.

Chapter 15: Golden Books

Marcus, Leonard. *Golden Legacy: The Story of Golden Books*. Golden Books, 2007.

Marcus, Leonard. *Minders of Make Believe*. Houghton Mifflin, 2008.

Patterson, Francine. *Koko's Kitten*. Scholastic, 1987.

Silvey, Anita. *Children's Book-a-Day Almanac*. 22 March 2011, http://childrensbookalmanac .com/2011/03/busy-busy-town.

Silvey Anita. *Everything I Need to Know I Learned from a Children's Book*. Roaring Brook, 2009.

Chapter 16: The H. A. and Margret Rey Collection

McKenzie, Muriel. "Curious George Stirs Young Minds." *Patriot Ledger*, November 1980, H. A. and Margret Rey Papers, de Grummond Children's Literature Collection, University of Southern Mississippi, box 72, folder 5.

Rey, H. A. Letter to Ursula Nordstrom. 5 March 1973. MS. H. A. and Margret Rey Papers, de Grummond Children's Literature Collection, University of Southern Mississippi, box 50, folder 5.

Chapter 18: Other Notable de Grummond Collections

Allison, Alida, and Tana Hoban. "'I' of the Beholder: An Interview with Tana Hoban." *The Lion and the Unicorn*, vol. 24, no. 1, 2000, pp. 143–49.

Blankstein, Amy. "Tana Hoban Transformed Children as Subjects and Seers." *ASMP Bulletin*, vol. 24, no. 4, 2006, p. 33.

Fichtner, Margaria. "70 Years to Draw On." *Miami Herald*, 15 July 1983, p. 1B.

Flor, Dorothy-Anne. "Writing to Make Children Laugh." *Fort Lauderdale News*, 21 November 1982, pp. 38SL–40SL (405–7).

Marshall, James. Letter to Dee Jones. 27 March 1987. James Marshall Papers, de Grummond Children's Literature Collection, University of Southern Mississippi, Hattiesburg.

Marshall, James. Letter to Dee Jones. 8 June 1987. James Marshall Papers, de Grummond Children's Literature Collection, University of Southern Mississippi, Hattiesburg.

Telgen, Diane. *Something about the Author. Facts and Pictures about Authors and Illustrators of Books for Young People*, vol. 75, Gale, 1994.

CONTRIBUTORS

ANN MULLOY ASHMORE is an associate professor of library services at Delta State University. Her interest in the lives of the Reys began in 2000 as a collection specialist at de Grummond. She has published articles about the Reys in both scholarly journals and popular periodicals. Most recently she collaborated on *Monkey Business: The Adventures of Curious George's Creators*, a 2017 documentary film about H. A. and Margret Rey.

RUDINE SIMS BISHOP is professor emerita of education at The Ohio State University, where she taught children's literature. She is the author of several books, including *Shadow and Substance: Afro-American Experience in Contemporary Children's Fiction* (1982), *Presenting Walter Dean Myers* (1990), *Kaleidoscope: A Multicultural Booklist for Grades K–8* (1994), and *Wonders: The Best Children's Poems of Effie Lee Newsome* (1999).

RUTH B. BOTTIGHEIMER, research professor in the Department of English at Stony Brook University and a historian of European fairy tales, has published *Magic Tales and Fairy Tale Magic from Ancient Egypt to Renaissance Italy* (2014), *Fairy Tales Framed* (2012), *Fairy Tales: A New History* (2009), *Fairy Godfather: Straparola, Venice, and the Fairy Tale Tradition* (2002), *The Bible for Children* (1996), *Grimm's Bad Girls and Bold Boys: The Moral and Social Vision of the Tales* (1987), and *Fairy Tales and Society: Illusion, Allusion, and Paradigm* (1987).

JENNIFER BRANNOCK is professor and curator of Rare Books and Mississippiana at the University of Southern Mississippi. She has a BA in art history and a MSLS from the University of Kentucky. Her research interests include popular culture, special collections outreach and reference, and gender and sexuality in midcentury sleaze publications.

CAROLYN J. BROWN is a writer, editor, and independent scholar, whose publications include articles in *Notes on Mississippi Writers*, *College Language Journal*, *Persuasions: The Jane Austen Journal*, and the *Eudora Welty Review*, as well as three biographies: *A Daring Life: A Biography of Eudora Welty* (2012), *Song of My Life: A Biography of Margaret Walker* (2014), and *The Artist's Sketch: A Biography of Painter Kate Freeman Clark* (2017).

RAMONA CAPONEGRO is an associate professor of children's literature at Eastern Michigan University. Drawing from archival research, she has published articles about the Ezra Jack Keats Book Award, early readers, and representations of juvenile delinquency in children's literature. She is the chair of the 2019 Pura Belpré Award Committee and the 2019–2021 Phoenix Picture Book Award Committee, and is actively involved in the University of Southern Mississippi's Fay B. Kaigler Children's Book Festival.

LORINDA COHOON is an associate professor in the Department of English at the University of Memphis, where she teaches graduate and undergraduate courses in children's literature. Her research focuses on children's periodicals. She completed her PhD at the University of Southern Mississippi, where she made use of the rich resources of the de Grummond Collection on an almost daily basis.

Speaker and author CAROL EDMONSTON is the niece of Syd Hoff. Since Hoff's passing in 2004, it has been her mission to preserve his rich and diverse legacy by creating the website www.SydHoff.org, and establishing the Syd Hoff Research Fellowship Endowment at the University of Southern Mississippi.

Paige Gray approaches the study of children's and young adult literature as a means to explore questions of voice, agency, and creative expression. Her book *Cub Reporters: American Children's Literature and Journalism in the Golden Age* (2019) considers the cultural and historical intersections between books for young people and newspapers in the late nineteenth and early twentieth centuries. She teaches at the Savannah College of Art and Design in Atlanta.

Laura Hakala is an assistant professor of English at the University of North Carolina at Pembroke, where she teaches composition and American literature. Her articles on Southern girlhood have appeared in *Children's Literature, Children's Literature Association Quarterly*, and the *Southern Quarterly*.

Andrew Haley is an associate professor at the University of Southern Mississippi. His first book, *Turning the Tables: American Restaurant Culture and the Rise of the Middle Class, 1880–1920*, won the 2012 James Beard Award for Scholarship and Reference. He is currently working on a book that explores how Mississippi community cookbooks tell the story of changing race relations, gender politics, and American nationalism in the twentieth century.

Wm John Hare is the co-owner with his wife Jill of Cellar Door Books in Bow, New Hampshire, and coauthor with Priscilla Hare of *Tasha Tudor: The Direction of Her Dreams*.

Dee Jones (Dolores Blythe Jones) was curator of the de Grummond Children's Literature Collection for nearly twenty years, beginning in 1986.

Allison G. Kaplan is faculty associate in the Information School, University of Wisconsin–Madison. She was the recipient of the 2017 Ezra Jack Keats/Janina Domanska Fellowship for which she conducted research on Tana Hoban using Hoban's papers in the de Grummond Collection. Her research includes the history of children's literature, mindfulness in children's literature, and early literacy.

MEGAN NORCIA is an associate professor at SUNY College at Brockport whose research and teaching interests focus on empire and nineteenth-century children's literary and material culture. She has written about imperial geography in *X Marks the Spot: Women Writers Map the Empire for British Children, 1790–1895* (2010) and imperialism in children's games in *The Imperial Agenda of Children's Board Games* (2019). She is happiest when up to her elbows in archives.

NATHALIE OP DE BEECK is an associate professor of English at Pacific Lutheran University and is the author of *Suspended Animation: Children's Picture Books and the Fairy Tale of Modernity* (2010) and cocreator of *Little Machinery: A Critical Facsimile Edition* (2009). Her scholarly interests include picture books, graphic narrative, and environmental studies.

AMY PATTEE is an associate professor in the School of Library and Information Science at Simmons University in Boston, where she teaches courses related to children's and young adult literature for students in the university's graduate program in library and information science as well as in its graduate programs in children's literature. She is a lover of series fiction and is especially fond of Trixie Belden.

As executive director, DEBORAH POPE has focused the work and mission of the Ezra Jack Keats Foundation on increasing diversity in children's literature and enriching the quality of public education. In partnership with the de Grummond Children's Literature Collection, she has extended recognition of the Ezra Jack Keats Book Award as an imprimatur of quality children's books for a diverse audience, nationally and internationally.

ELLEN HUNTER RUFFIN, associate professor, has been the curator of the de Grummond Children's Literature Collection since 2006. She has chaired the Arbuthnot Lecture Committee and served on the Newbery Medal Committee, the Children's Literature Legacy Award Committee (previously the Laura Ingalls Wilder Award), the Phoenix Picture Book Award Committee, and the Schneider Family Book Award Committee of the American Library Association.

ANITA SILVEY is the former editor of *Horn Book Magazine* and publisher of children's books at Houghton Mifflin. She has published six critical volumes about children's books, including *Children's Books and Their Creators*, *100 Best Books for Children*, *Everything I Need to Know I Learned from a Children's Book*, and the *Children's Book-a-Day Almanac*. She teaches history of children's book publishing at Simmons University.

DANIELLE BISHOP STOULIG is currently a children's librarian in Baton Rouge, Louisiana. She is a former assistant curator at the de Grummond Collection, where she was a member of the staff for eighteen years. She always said that the best part of her job at de Grummond was being able to hold in her hands the original manuscripts and artwork from children's books. Now, being able to place the published version of these books into the hands of young readers on a daily basis makes her feel pretty special.

ROGER SUTTON has been editor in chief, The Horn Book, Inc., since 1996. He has an MA from the Graduate Library School, University of Chicago, and worked in public libraries through the 1980s. With Martha V. Parravano, he is the author of *A Family of Readers*, published in 2010 by Candlewick Press.

DEBORAH D. TAYLOR joined the Enoch Pratt Free Library in 1974 and recently retired from there as coordinator of school and student services. She has served on numerous book and library services committees, including the Sibert Award Committee for Outstanding Informational Books, the Printz Award Committee, and the Newbery Award Committee. She also chaired the Coretta Scott King Book Awards Committee. In 2015 she received the 2015 Coretta Scott King–Virginia Hamilton Award for Lifetime Achievement from the American Library Association.

ERIC L. TRIBUNELLA, professor of English, teaches children's and young adult literature at the University of Southern Mississippi. He is the author of *Melancholia and Maturation: The Use of Trauma in American Children's Literature* (2010), coauthor of *Reading Children's Literature: A Critical Introduction* (2013, 2019), and editor of a critical edition of Edward Prime-Stevenson's *Left to Themselves* (1891/2016).

ALEXANDRA VALINT is an associate professor of English at the University of Southern Mississippi. She researches and teaches Victorian literature, children's and young-adult literature, and narrative theory. She is the author of *Narrative Bonds: Multiple Narrators in the Victorian Novel* (2021), and her publications have appeared in journals such as *Victorian Literature and Culture*; *Dickens Studies Annual*; *English Literature in Transition, 1880–1920*; and *Children's Literature Association Quarterly*.

LAURA E. WASOWICZ is curator of children's literature at the American Antiquarian Society. Since 1987 she has worked to acquire, catalog, and provide reference service for the AAS collection of 27,000 American children's books issued between 1650 and 1899. She is the coauthor of *Radiant with Color & Art: McLoughlin Brothers and the Business of Picture Books, 1858–1920* (2017).

Index

Page numbers in **boldface** indicate illustrations.

folk tales, 28, 30, 30n2, 103
Forbes, Steve, 98
Ford, Miela Hoban, 109
"Fox in the Grapes, The" (Aesop), 26
Fox on Stage (James Marshall), 115
frame story/tale, 26, 76
Francis Forrester's Boys' and Girls' Magazine, 62
Frank Reade Library series (Tousey), 49
Frederick Warne and Co., 35, 71
Freedom Summer (Wiles), 88
Freeman, Don, 90
Frog Prince, The (Crane), 68

Gaither Sisters series (Garcia-Williams), 52
galleys, 8, 18, 112, 115
Gallimard, 100
games, xiii–xiv, 45, 65, 67–68, 71
gender, 66, 84; and address, 49, 51–52; and boyhood, 56, 58; and expectations of boys and girls, 75–76; of readers, 49
General Electric, 110
George, Sean, 23
George and Martha (James Marshall), 115
George and Martha series, 115
Gergely, Tibor, 97
ghostwriters, 51, 53, 113
Giant Golden Book of Mathematics, The (Adler), 99
Giant Golden Books, 99
Giblin, James Cross, 78
G.I. Joe, 67
Girl's Own Paper, xiii, 62, **63**
Glory Be (Scattergood), 88
Goggles (Keats), 107
Golden, Catherine, 41
Golden Bible for Children: The New Testament, The (Werner), 98
Golden Book of Science for Boys and Girls, The (Parker), 98
Golden Books, xv, 66, 95–99
Golden Egg Book, The (M. W. Brown), 97
Golden Guides series, 79

Goodman, Andrew, 6–7
Goodnight Moon (M. W. Brown), 97
Gottlieb, William P., 76
Goulding, Francis Robert, 86
Grandfather's Journey (Say), 113
graphic narratives, 73
graphic novels, 93
Great Round World and What Is Going On in It, 62
Green, Hank, 93
Green, John, xiv, 84, 92–93, **92**
Greenaway, Kate, xiii, 22, **34**, 35, 41, 45–47, **46**, 70
Greene, Carla, 76
Greer, Glyndon Flynt, 82
Greetham, David, 54
Grimm, Jacob and Wilhelm, 28
Grimms' collection of tales, 30, 67
Gullah-Geechee, 88

Haas, Dorothy, 112
Hader, Berta and Elmer, 9, **10**, 11, 72
Hail Mary, 31
"Half a Century of U.S. Photography," 109
Hamilton, Mary, 23
Hardy Boys series, 51, 52
Hare, Wm John and Priscilla T. Collection, 112
Harper Books for Boys and Girls, 97, 101. *See also* HarperCollins
HarperCollins, 110. *See also* Harper Books for Boys and Girls
Harriet the Spy (Fitzhugh), 89, 90
Harris, Joel Chandler, 87, **88**
Harry Potter series, 67, 68, 74, 94
Hattiesburg, Mississippi, 4–5, 9, 11–12, **13**, 20–21, 24, 104, 137
Hawthorne, Nathaniel, 112
Hazel (Ovington), 87
Highlights Foundation, 91
Hill, Margaret Ohler, 20
Hinton, S. E., 91

Histoires, ou Contes du temps passé (Perrault), 27–28
historical fiction, 93, 94, 113
Hitchcock, Alfred, 110
Hoban, Tana, xv, 109–10, **126, 127**
Hoff, Syd (Sydney Hoffberg), xv, 16, 93, 110–11, **128**
Hogarth, Grace, 56, 101
Holl, Adelaide, 20
Holmes, Efner, 112
Hoole, Charles, 55, **55**, 56
Horn Book, xv, 80, 81, 82
hornbooks, xiii, 31–33, **32**, 70
Houghton Mifflin, 101, 114
Houma, Louisiana, 4
House That Jack Built, The (Caldecott), **44**, 45
Howdy Doody, 99
How to Behave and How to Amuse (Sandison), 67, **68**
How to Have What You Want in Your Future (L. de Grummond), 18
Hughes, Langston, 80, **81**
Hughes, Thomas, 68
Hunt, Peter, 37
Hurd, Edith Thacher, 77, 97

I Can Fly (Krauss), 98
I Can Read! series, 93, 110
Idle, Molly, 68
illustrations, xiii, xvi, 5, 6, 11, 12, 13, 22, 23, 32, 41–42, 44–47, 55–56, 79, 82, 90, 95, 97, 101, 103, 104, 108, 112, 115, 134
illustrators, xi–xiii, 5–9, 12, 16, 21, 22–23, 35, 41, 46–47, 72, 82, 91, 95, 97, 105, 107, 110, 132, 134, 136–37
"Image of the Black in Children's Fiction" (Baker), 80
Index to the Youth's Companion, 62
informational books, 56, 74, 78
International Federation of Library Associations, 23
issues books, 90
I Want to Be a Space Pilot (Greene), 76, 78

Rojankovsky, Feodor, 97
Rollins, Charlemae Hill, 81
Rollo series, xiii, 48, **49**
Rowling, J. K., 67, 94
Royal Primer, The, **38**
Rylant, Cynthia, 88

Sabuda, Robert, 68
Sad-Faced Boy, The (E. K. Evans with
    Hughes), 80
Saggy Baggy Elephant, The (Jackson), 96
Sailor Dog, The (M. W. Brown), 97, **98**
Sammy the Seal (Hoff), 110
Sanders, Joe Sutliff, 80
Sanders' Union Reader (Sanders), 36, **37**
Sandison, George Henry, 67
Saturday Evening Post, 110
Say, Allen, 113
Scarry, Richard, 95, 97
Scattergood, Augusta, 88
Schiffrin, Jacques, 100
Schleger, Hans, 103
Schneider, Leo, 16
school stories, 94
Schwebel, Sarah L., 94
Schwerner, Michael, 7
Scott O'Dell Award, 113
Scribner's Illustrated Classics, 47
Scruffy the Tugboat (Gergely), 97
Secret Garden, The (Burnett), xiii, 54, 56
self-publishing, 91
Sendak, Maurice, 45, 69, 93, 135
serialized stories, 49, 87
series fiction, viii, xiii, 48, 49, 51, 52
Sesame Street, 99
Seuss, Dr., 93, 97
Seventeen Cookbook, The, 76
17th Street Productions, 51–52
Shepard, E. H., 21, 120
Shilling Toy Books series, 68
Siegelson, Kim, 88
Sign of the Cross, 31, 32
Simon & Schuster, 95

sketchbooks, 114
slavery, 84, 137
Slave's Friend, The, 62
"Sleeping Beauty," 28
Slobodkina, Esphyr, xii, 72, **124**
Snowy Day, The (Keats), xv, 73, 74, 90, 105,
    106, 108, **121**, 136
Sobol, Donald, 18
social class, 84
Society of Children's Book Writers and
    Illustrators, 23, 91
Southern Primer, The, 36, 39, **85**
Southern Quarterly, The, 88
Space Flight and How It Works (Gottlieb), 76
special collections, 32, 65, 131
Spotty (M. Rey), 101
Stars: A New Way to See Them, The (H. A.
    Rey), **103**
Stevenson, Robert Louis, 47
St. Nicholas, xiii, **60**, 62, 64
Stolz, Mary, 91
Story of Dr. Dolittle, The (Lofting), 55
Story of King Arthur and His Knights, The
    (Pyle), 47
Straparola, Giovan Francesco, 27, **28**
Stratego, 67
Stratemeyer, Edward, 51, 52
Stratemeyer Literary Syndicate, 51, 53
Strawberry Girl (Lenski), 21, 88
Street and Smith, 49
Stuart Little (White), 11
Student and Schoolmate, 62
Stupids, The (Allard and Marshall), 115
Sweet Pea (Krementz), 88, 141
Sweet Valley High series, 51, 52

Tales of Hoff (Hoff), 110
Tasha Tudor: The Direction of Her Dreams
    (Hare and Hare), 112
Tawny Scrawny Lion (Jackson), 96
Taylor, Mildred, 88
Teenage Mutant Ninja Turtles, 99
teetotum, 67

Tenggren, Gustaf, 95, 96, **99**
Tenniel, John, 46
Three Jovial Huntsmen, The (Caldecott), 45
Three Little Kittens, The, 98
Tim All Alone (Ardizzone), 72
Time, 109
Toby Tyler; or, Ten Weeks with a Circus
    (Otis), 56, **58**
Tolkien, J. R. R., 11
Tom Brown's Schooldays (Hughes), 68
Tom Swift series, 51, 52
*Tony Sarg's Surprise Book: Look, Listen,
    Smell, Taste, Feel* (Sarg), 68
Tougaloo College, 6
Tousey, Frank, 49
toy books, xiii, 68
toys, xiii, xiv, 65, 66, 67, 68, 71
Toy Story franchise, 66
translation, 27, 28, **30**, 55
Trapped! A Whale's Rescue (Burleigh), **125**
Treasure Island (Stevenson), 47
Trites, Roberta Seelinger, 91
Tudor, Bethany, 112
Tudor, Rosamond, 112
Tudor, Tasha, xv, 111, 112, **129**
Tupi, 103
Tuthill, Louisa, 86
Twain, Mark, 91
typescript, xii, 8, 19, 90, 93, 112
*Types of International Folktale: A Classifica-
    tion and Bibliography* (Uther), 30

Under the Window (Greenaway), 45
United States Board on Books for Young
    People, 23
Universe, The (Zim), 56, 79
University of Louisiana–Lafayette, 3
University of Munich, 100
University of Southern Mississippi, 3, 4, 5,
    9, 11, 13, 19, 21, 73, 104, 108, **120**, 131, 132,
    133, 134
University of Southern Mississippi Medal-
    lion, 132